7+ MATHS, VOLUME 2

Practice Papers & In-Depth Answers

R. P. DAVIS

Copyright © 2022 Accolade Tuition Ltd
Published by Accolade Tuition Ltd
71-75 Shelton Street
Covent Garden
London WC2H 9JQ
www.accoladetuition.com
info@accoladetuition.com

The right of R. P. Davis to be identified as the author of this work has been asserted by him in accordance with the Copyright, Designs and Patents Act 1988.

All rights reserved. No part of this book may be reproduced in any form or by any electronic or mechanical means, including information storage and retrieval systems, without written permission from the author, except for the use of brief quotations in a book review.

ISBN: 978-1-913988-32-6

FIRST EDITION

1 3 5 7 9 10 8 6 4 2

Contents

Foreword	1

Paper One: The All-Rounder Paper

The All-Rounder Paper	9
Model Answers & Guidance	17

Paper Two: The Short and Sweet Paper

The Short and Sweet Paper	37
Model Answers & Guidance	43

Paper Three: The Application Paper

The Application Paper	57
Model Answers & Guidance	65

Paper Four: The Number and Calculation Paper

The Number and Calculation Paper	81
Model Answers & Guidance	91

Paper Five: The Incremental Calculation Paper

The Incremental Calculation Paper	113
Model Answers & Guidance	125

Paper Six: The Bit Of Everything Paper

The Bit Of Everything Paper	149
Model Answers & Guidance	159

Paper Seven: The Multi-Parts, Multi-Steps Paper

The Multi-Parts, Multi-Steps Paper	175
Model Answers & Guidance	189

Paper Eight: The Thematic Paper

The Thematic Paper 213
Model Answers & Guidance 227

Foreword

When sitting 7+ Maths exams at top schools you will notice that, although all of their papers cover similar ground, the *types* of questions they ask can vary a good deal. The reason for this is simple enough: these schools write their papers in-house, and that means you find quirks in some papers that you don't in others. And yet, for all these quirks, there is still a *huge* degree of overlap between these various papers, because ultimately these schools are all looking for a similar set of skills.

As a result, preparing for these exams is eminently possible. We simply need to identify the various types of questions that appear (including those quirky ones!), then hone the skills required to answer them.

The intention of this guide is not simply to show you what these exams tend to look like (although, as you work through it, you will inevitably get a sense of this nonetheless!). No, the intention is to go a step further, and show you how to decode the sorts of questions these 7+ Maths papers tend to ask. Moreover, it also seeks to explain, *in detail*, how the answers provided were calculated, so students can feel confident emulating the methods.

While we are shortly going to delve into the specific questions that appear in these papers, it is important to briefly note here that all schools base their questions on the objectives for Years 2 and 3 students set out in the Maths National Curriculum – these schools are ultimately looking to see how well a candidate can apply skills they've learned in class when confronted with potentially unfamiliar questions.

How this book is set out.

As mentioned, 7+ papers are incredibly varied. However, if you spend enough time and energy looking through past papers, you start to figure out what makes them tick, and notice certain patterns that emerge time and again. This book contains eight papers, each written in a different "style" – and each style reflects a different type of paper one might encounter in a 7+ Maths exam. I have labelled the eight types of papers as follows:

1. The All-Rounder Paper
2. The Short and Sweet Paper
3. The Application Paper
4. The Number and Calculation Paper
5. The Incremental Calculation Paper
6. The Bit of Everything Paper
7. The Multi-Parts, Multi-Steps Paper
8. The Thematic Paper

The labels I've given each style should give you some indication of what the papers entail. It may well be the case that some of the 7+ Maths papers you end up taking fit neatly into one of these styles. However, it is just as possible that they wind up being a blend of two (or more) styles – after all, schools often tweak the style of paper they put out year on year.

At any rate, I can assert with confidence that, if you are well versed in all eight styles, you will have your bases covered, and be prepared for most anything.

The questions for each paper appear twice. The first time they will appear by themselves, so that students can, if they wish, have a go at tackling the paper. They will then appear a second time, but this time accompanied by answers and detailed guidance.

Each of the papers includes a "time guide" – that is, the amount of time one would expect to be given to complete the paper in an exam hall. If students wish to complete some of these papers as practice, I suspect this may prove useful.

Insofar as difficulty is concerned, these papers have been ordered from easiest to hardest. The truth of the matter is that 7+ exam papers are *not* uniform in difficulty: some schools set harder papers than others – and these discrepancies in difficulty exist even between top-flight schools whose papers you might expect to be pretty similar.

I feel the need at this point to clarify that my intention is *not* to intimidate by saying this. On the contrary, by exposing students to the reality of what is in store, I believe it ensures that, when it actually comes to entering the exam hall, you feel far more at ease.

There is no *correct* way to use this guide, though I would suggest it is probably sensible to have a parent at hand to act as a kind of surrogate tutor while the student works through this volume. In any case, the intention of this book is to give the reader the experience of having an experienced tutor at their beck and call.

Tips

Within this book, you will find a good deal of question specific advice. However, there are a few more general mathematical tips that it is important for any 7+ candidate to keep in mind:

- Remember to underline key words in word problems.
- Recap all vocabulary associated with each calculation symbol: + - ÷ x
- Check your work: for example, students can check their answers to calculations by doing the inverse operation (opposite operation – subtraction/addition or multiplication/division).

For all operations, if you are missing the first number, you need to do the inverse (opposite) operation:

$\_ + 6 = 10 \implies 10 - 6 = \underline{4}$

$\_ - 4 = 7 \implies 7 + 4 = \underline{11}$

$\_ \times 3 = 15 \implies 15 \div 3 = \underline{5}$

$\_ \div 2 = 6 \implies 6 \times 2 = \underline{12}$

If you are missing the middle number, for addition and subtraction you subtract, and for multiplication and division you divide:

$8 + \_ = 14 \implies 14 - 8 = \underline{6}$

$20 - \_ = 10 \implies 20 - 10 = \underline{10}$

$4 \times \_ = 8 \implies 8 \div 4 = \underline{2}$

$30 \div \_ = 3 \implies 30 \div 3 = \underline{10}$

- Remember that adding and subtracting 10 from a given two-digit number can be a great way to make your life easier. Use this knowledge to help you when adding or subtracting 8 and 9 from a given number. For example, if you are asked to solve:

  57 – 9 =

You could mentally work out 57 − 10 = 47 and then add 1 at the end which would make the answer 48.

The same can be done if you need to take away 8. For example,
91 - 8 =

You would do 91 − 10 = 81 and then add 2 (=83).

If you are asked to add 8 or 9 to a given number, you would add 10 and then take away 1 or 2 at the end.

- When presented with a subtraction based question that requires you to use mental arithmetic, think carefully about which method to use. Take the following question:

  56 − 48 =

  Some children would take away 40 from 56 (=16) and then 8 from 16 (=8) but that method requires two steps/calculations.

  As 56 and 48 are so close together, it makes much more sense to simply count the difference between the two numbers − to get from 48 to 56, I do two jumps to 50 and then another six jumps, which makes eight jumps in total.

Paper One: The All-Rounder Paper

The All-Rounder Paper explores every topic within the maths curriculum – that is, place values, calculations, fractions, shapes, numbers, and measurements (times, capacities and sizes!).

There are 19 questions in this paper, worth a total of 33 marks. This paper has been placed at the start because it is the least time pressurised of all the papers in this edition. Not only are students given 60 minutes to complete this paper, but there are, compared to other papers in this guide, relatively few questions in total.

The All-Rounder Paper
60 MINUTES: 19 QUESTIONS, 33 MARKS

1. Work out the total of these three numbers? (1)

40   27   9

Answer: _____

2. Draw a circle around the even numbers floating in my Number Soup. (1)

3. Can you help Mr Wise Owl complete the calculations below using <, > or =. (3)

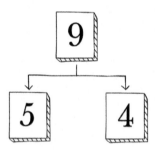

4. Here is one way for the number 9 to be partitioned: (1)

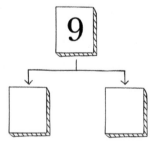

Can you find another way?

5. Peter Piper bought these four peppers for 16p. How much would five peppers cost? (1)

Answer: _____

6. Hemini played cards with her father for half an hour. When they finished, the time shown on the clock was as follows.

What time did they start playing? Fill in your answer on this digital clock. (1)

7. Toby baked 80 cupcakes.

He sold 42 at the school fete.

He then gave this tray to his friend Alice.

How many cupcakes did Toby have left? (2)

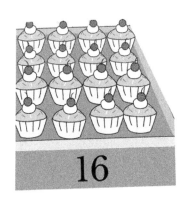

_____ **cupcakes**

8. Peter takes an afternoon nap. When he wakes up, his analogue clock is showing the time below. Write the same time on the digital clock. (1)

9. Look at the number line below. Fill in the fractions below. (1)

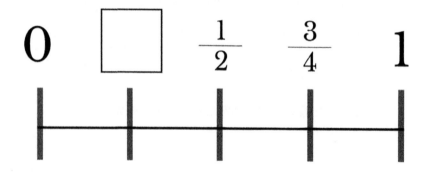

10. Here are some 3D shapes.

Tick the shape that has 5 faces.

Circle the shape that has 6 vertices. (2)

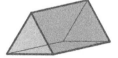

11. These pieces of rope are each 17 cm in length. They were cut from one long piece of rope.

How long was the original piece of rope? (1)

Answer: _____ cm

12. Maxine the Florist sold 7 red roses in the morning.

During the lunchtime rush, Maxine then sold three times more red roses.

Finally, just before closing her shop, Maxine sold 2 more red roses.

How many red roses did Maxine sell in total? (3)

_____ red roses

13. Mr Wise Owl has another test for you. Complete his calculations below. (4)

```
  43         88
+ 53       - 32
____       ____


 159        297
+ 33       - 49
____       ____
```

14. Fill in the missing number. (1)

$$8 + 5 = 6 + \boxed{}$$

15. The picture below shows how many mugs you could fill with one bag of coffee beans.

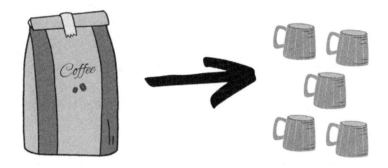

How many mugs could you fill if the bag of coffee beans was three times bigger? (1)

_____ mugs

16. Draw the hands on this clock to show what time it would be 15 minutes after 11 o'clock. (1)

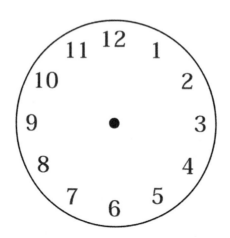

17. Here is a picture of some beetles.

Use this picture to help fill in the missing numbers. (3)

$$\Box \times 6 = 18$$

$$6 = \Box \div 3$$

$$6 + \Box + 6 = 18$$

18. Within the blank boxes, draw the next two pictures in the pattern. (2)

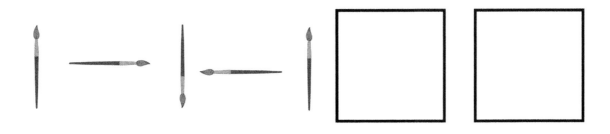

19. Ms. Li, the Headmistress of Lawndale School, surveyed her students, asking them to name their favourite subject. (3)

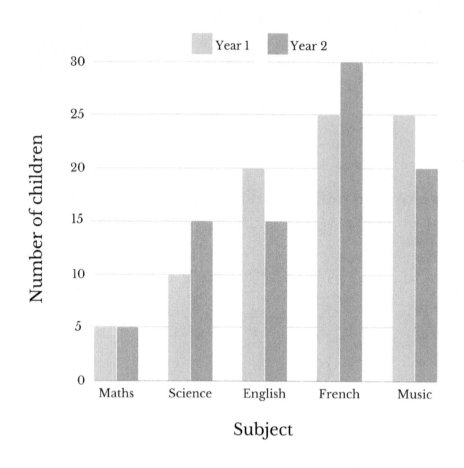

a. Which subject is the most popular?

Answer: _____

b. How many more students in Year 1 chose music as their favourite than in Year 2?

Answer: _____

c. How many students were questioned in this survey?

Answer: _____

Model Answers & Guidance

1. What is the total of these three numbers? (1)

40   27   9

Add up all the tens and all the ones separately, then add together the two totals.

Award one mark for the correct answer.

Answer: 76

2. Draw a circle around the even numbers floating in my Number Soup. (1)

Recap what is meant by even numbers (= numbers that can be halved into two equal parts – in other words, any number that ends in 0, 2, 4, and 8).

Award one mark for all even numbers being circled.

3. Can you help Mr Wise Owl complete the calculations below using <, > or =. (3)

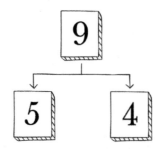

$32 + 5 \;\boxed{>}\; 29 + 6$

$5 \times 2 \;\boxed{<}\; 4 \times 3$

$18 - 4 \;\boxed{=}\; 19 - 5$

4. Here is one way for the number 9 to be partitioned: (1)

9
↙ ↘
5   4

Can you find another way?

Model Answers & Guidance

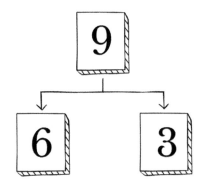

The challenge here is to find another pair of numbers that equal 9, and then to write these numbers into the empty box. This can be any pair other than the example already given in the question (for example, **'8 and 1'**, **or '7 and 2'**, **or '6 and 3' - which is the answer I offer above**).

5. Peter Piper bought these four peppers for 16p. How much would five peppers cost? (1)

This is a multi-step question.

First, if four peppers cost 16p, then we need to realise that we need to divide 16p by 4 in order to find the price of 1 pepper.

$16 \div 4 = 4p$

So one pepper costs 4p.

Next, to find the cost of five peppers, we need to multiply 4p by 5.

$4 \times 5 = 20p$

Therefore, the cost of 5 peppers is 20p

Answer: <u>20p or £0.20</u>

6. Hemini played cards with her father for half an hour. When they finished, the time shown on the clock was as follows.

08:05

What time did they start playing? Fill in your answer on this digital clock. (1)

Discuss with your child how many minutes there are in half an hour, and then ask: 'if the break ends at 10:30am, do we need to take away or add half an hour to the time?'.

Award one mark for the correct time.

7. Toby baked 80 cupcakes.

He sold 42 at the school fete.

He then gave this tray to his friend Alice.

How many cupcakes did Toby have left? (2)

$$80 - 42 = 38$$
$$38 - 16 = 22$$
So: 22 cupcakes remaining
OR
$$16 + 42 = 58$$
$$80 - 58 = 22$$
So: 22 cupcakes remaining

This is a multi-step question.

Above, I have shown two different methods of finding the answer. I'll explain them both below.

Method 1:

First, I subtracted 42 from 80, which gave me 38 — the number of cupcakes Toby had left after the school fete.

Next, I subtracted 16 from 38, which gave me 22 — the number of cupcakes Toby had left after he gave the tray to Alice.

This led me to a final answer of 22 cupcakes.

Method 2:

Now, let's look at my second method.

First, I added together the number of cupcakes Toby sold at the Fete (42) and the number he gave to Alice (16). This gave me a total of 58.

Next, I subtracted 58 from 80, the total number of Toby originally baked.

This again gave me 22 cupcakes.

Award 2 marks for the correct answer and take away a mark for each step that is incorrect.

Answer: 22 Cupcakes

8. Peter takes an afternoon nap. When he wakes up, his analogue clock is showing the time below. Write the same time on the digital clock. (1)

Remind your child that when we get near to the next hour (3), the hour hand is closer to 3 than to 2.

Award one mark for writing the correct time. If they write 14:45 (24 hour format) they should still be awarded the mark.

9. Look at the number line below. Fill in the fraction below. (1)

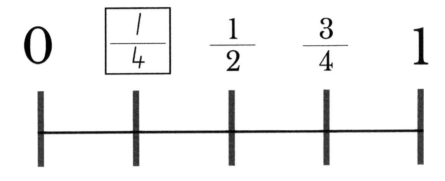

Each time we go up one step on the number line, we are going up by one quarter ¼.

We can test this by subtracting ¼ from 1 — the last number on the number line. This gives us ¾. This is indeed the next 'step' down on the number line.

Moreover, if we subtract ¼ from ¾, we get ½, which is the next 'step' down on the number line.

So to find the missing fraction — the second 'step' on the number line — all we need to do is add ¼ to 0, the very first number on the number line. This gives us ¼, the correct answer!

10. Here are some 3D shapes.

Tick the shape that has 5 faces.

Circle the shape that has 6 vertices. (2)

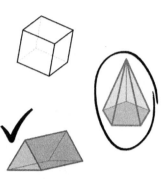

A face is the flat shape — so if we take the triangular prism (the bottom left shape) as an example, it has five faces in all: the three rectangular faces, and the two triangular faces on either side.

A vertex is the corner of a 3D shape – where two or more edges (lines) meet (the plural of vertex is vertices).

Although there are no marks for this, let's quickly consider the cube to the top left. It has 6 faces, and 8 vertices.

Award one mark for each correct answer.

11. These pieces of rope are each 17 cm in length. They were cut from one long piece of rope.

How long was the original piece of rope? (1)

The key with this question is to look at the picture and to notice that there are *four* pieces of rope. This means we need to add up 17cm four times. Your child may use the column method or write the numbers out in a 'traditional' calculation (horizontally). They may also choose to draw the calculation in their own way — perhaps by showing they are adding up all the tens and then all the ones.

$$\begin{array}{r}17\\17\\17\\+17\\\hline 68\\{\scriptstyle 2}\end{array}$$

Award one mark for the correct answer. If the candidate writes out their method of addition correctly, but gets the wrong answer, they will not secure the mark.

$$17 + 17 + 17 + 17 = 68$$

Answer: <u>68 cm</u>

12. Maxine the Florist sold 7 red roses in the morning.

During the lunchtime rush, Maxine then sold three times more red roses.

Finally, just before closing her shop, Maxine sold 2 more red roses.

How many red roses did Maxine sell in total? (3)

$$7 + 7 + 7 = 21 \quad OR \quad 7 \times 3 = 21$$

$$21 + 7 = 28$$

$$28 + 2 = 30$$

This is a multi-step question.

First your child needs to work out how many roses Maxine sold during the lunchtime rush multiplying 7 by 3.

Next, your child needs to add together the 7 roses in the morning, the 21 during the lunchtime rush, and the 2 just before closing.

Award 3 marks for the correct answer and take away a mark for each step that is incorrect.

Answer: 30

13. Mr Wise Owl has another test for you. Complete his calculations below. (4)

$$\begin{array}{r} 43 \\ +53 \\ \hline 96 \end{array} \qquad \begin{array}{r} 88 \\ -32 \\ \hline 56 \end{array}$$

$$\begin{array}{r} 159 \\ +33 \\ \hline 192 \\ \scriptstyle 1 \end{array} \qquad \begin{array}{r} \scriptstyle 8 \\ 2\cancel{9}7 \\ -49 \\ \hline 248 \end{array}$$

TOP LEFT: this question is straightforward – your child simply needs to add 3 and 3 (=6); then they need to add 4(0) to make 5(0) (=9(0)).

TOP RIGHT: First, we subtract 2 from 8 = 6. Next, we subtract 3(0) from 8(0) = 5(0).

BOTTOM LEFT: add 9 and 3 (=12). Put the one under the tens section, and then add 5(0), 3(0) and 1(0). Finally, we do not need to add anything to 1(00).

BOTTOM RIGHT: we are not able to subtract 9 from 7 without entering into negative numbers, therefore it is clear that you need to borrow a ten from 'next door'. We then subtract 9 from 17 (=8). Next, we simply subtract 4(0) from 8(0) = 4(0). Finally, we subtract zero from 2(00). Encourage your child to double check their answers when they are done!

Award one mark for each correct answer.

14. Fill in the missing number. (1)

$$8 + 5 = 6 + \boxed{7}$$

The first step here is to work out 8 + 5 (=13).

We then need to add a number to 6 so that we end up with 13.

To find this number, we simply subtract 6 from 13.

13 - 6 = 7.

As a result, we know our answer is 7.

Answer: 7

15. The picture below shows how many mugs you could fill with one bag of coffee beans.

How many mugs could you fill if the bag of coffee beans was three times bigger? (1)

We can see in the image that the bag of coffee contains enough beans to fill up 5 mugs.

If the bag is three times bigger, we know that it will be able to fill up <u>three times as many mugs.</u>

So we need to multiply 5 by 3, which gives us 15. This is our answer!

Answer: <u>15 mugs</u>

16. Draw the hands on this clock to show what time it would be 15 minutes after 11 o'clock. (1)

The minute (longer) hand moves clockwise from number to number every five minutes, starting at 12.

As a result, when it is 15 minutes past any hour — be it 4 o'clock, 8 o'clock, or 11 o'clock — the minute hand will always be pointing at the number 3.

The hour (smaller) hand moves clockwise between each number every sixty minutes. As a result, if we are a quarter hour past 11 o'clock, the hour hand will be one quarter of the way towards 12, but will for the moment still be nearer to 11.

17. Here is a picture of some beetles.

Use this picture to help fill in the missing numbers. (3)

$$\boxed{3} \times 6 = 18$$

$$6 = \boxed{18} \div 3$$

$$6 + \boxed{6} + 6 = 18$$

The picture presents us with 3 beetles, each with 6 legs. Between them, we can count 18 legs.

Students can use this observation to help them fill in the blanks, though some students may not need the image to help them do so.

TOP: The top sum is basically asking us, what number do we need to multiply by 6 to get 18. We know from the image that if we multiply 6 legs by 3, we get 18, so from this we can infer that the answer is 3

Alternatively, we can simply work it out by dividing 18 by 6, which also gives us 3.

MIDDLE: What number, when divided by 3, will gives us 6?

Well, to work this out, we simply need to multiply 6 by 3.

We know from the image that if we multiply 6 legs by 3, we get 18, which is the correct answer.

BOTTOM: Which number, when added to two sixes, gives us 18?

Well, we know that 2 x 6 = 12. So to find the missing number, we simply need to subtract 12 from 18, which gives us 6.

Equally, we could see that each beetle has 6 legs, and when we add all 3, we get 18. As such, we know that the missing number must be 6.

18. Within the blank boxes, draw the next two pictures in the pattern. (2)

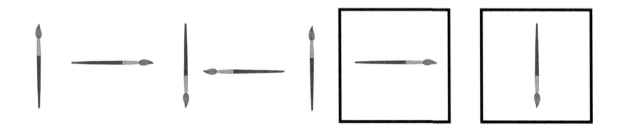

Model Answers & Guidance

Before anything else, it is important to recap with the student what the word 'clockwise' means and then review what we mean by a quarter turn, half turn, three quarter turn and full turn. A good activity that helps consolidate this idea is to get the student to stand and move in quarter turns (as shown in the diagram below), explaining how a half is the same as two quarters. You could also cut out shapes and practice rotating them.

If we look at the shape in question, we see that each time we go forward in the sequence, the paintbrush turns 90 degrees to the right (clockwise) — in other words, a quarter turn.

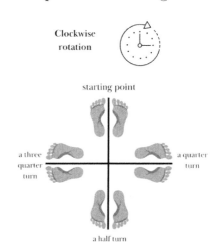

So the student needs to continue the pattern. The first blank box needs to have a paintbrush pointing rightwards (a 90 degree rightward turn from the upwards facing brush just before it). Then the final blank box needs to have a paintbrush pointing downwards.

19. Ms. Li, the Headmistress of Lawndale School, surveyed her students, asking them to name their favourite subject. (3)

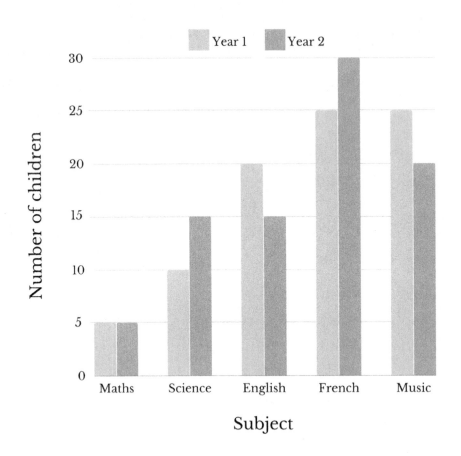

a. Which subject is the most popular?

French is the joint most popular subject for students in Year 1. And French is the most popular subject for students in Year 2. As a result, we can see that French is the most popular subject all in all.

Answer: French

b. How many more students in Year 1 chose music as their favourite than in Year 2?

In Year 1, we can see that 25 students chose Music as their favourite subject.

In Year 2, we can see that 20 students chose Music as their favourite subject.

To figure how many more chose Music from Year 1 when compared with Year 2, we simply subtract 20 from 25.

25 - 20 = 5.

Answer: 5 students

c. How many students were questioned in this survey?

Our first step is to work out how many students from each year chose each subject.

5 students chose Maths from Year 1, and 5 students chose Maths from Year 2.

So 5 + 5 = 10 students all in all chose Maths.

10 students chose Science from Year 1, and 15 students chose Science from Year 2.

So 10 + 15 = 25 students chose Science all in all.

20 students chose English from Year 1, and 15 students chose English from Year 2.

So 20 + 15 = 35 students chose English all in all.

25 students chose French from Year 1, and 30 students chose French from Year 2.

So 25 + 30 = 55 students chose French all in all.

25 students chose Music from Year 1, and 20 students chose Music from Year 2.

So 25 + 20 = 45 students chose Music all in all.

We then need to add together the students who selected each subject.

10 + 25 + 35 + 55 + 45 = 170

```
  1 0
  2 5
  3 5
  5 5
+ 4 5
-----
1 7 0
  2
```

The student may find it easier to use the column method to add these numbers.

Answer: 170

Paper Two: The Short and Sweet Paper

I have labeled this paper The Short and Sweet Paper as it is the shortest paper in this volume. However, while this paper contains just 14 questions, they cover a range of areas — including number and place value, calculations, fractions, geometry, time, word problems and statistics. Your child has 30 minutes to complete this paper, and there are 53 marks at stake.

The Short and Sweet Paper
30 MINUTES: 14 QUESTIONS, 53 MARKS

1. Fill in the missing number sequences below: (2)

___, 144, 148, 152, ___, ___

80, ___, 70, ___, 60, ___, 50, ___

2. Match the additions to the multiplications. One has already been completed for you. (3)

7 x 7   8 + 8 + 8 + 8 + 8 + 8

9 x 4   7 + 7 + 7 + 7 + 7 + 7 + 7

6 x 8   4 + 4 + 4 + 4 + 4

5 x 4   9 + 9 + 9 + 9

(7 x 7 is matched to 7 + 7 + 7 + 7 + 7 + 7 + 7)

3. Place the numbers in the cloud in the correct position so that all the numbers are in order of largest to smallest. (3)

902		397		313		20
largest						smallest

4. Use each card once to make the smallest total possible. (1)

3 6 7 8

☐☐ + ☐☐

5. Work out the following: (4)

a) 57 - 24 = _____

b) 85 - 56 = _____

c) 23 + 75 = _____

d) 19 + 69 = _____

6. Amit wants to set the time on his new wristwatch.

His digital clock is showing the time in the picture below.

Draw the hands on the analogue wristwatch below so that it shows the same time. (2)

7. Buffy the Beaver has a piece of wood.

It is 4 metres and 20 cm in length.

She breaks it into 3 equal pieces.

How long is each piece? (1)

Answer: _____m _____cm

8. Fill in the missing numbers: (3)

a) ¼ of 20 = ½ of ____

b) ½ of 12 = ¼ of ____

c) ⅓ of 15 = ¼ of ____

9. Fill in the missing numbers: (4)

a) ½ of 36 is ____

b) ½ of 44 is ____

c) Double 17 is ____

d) Double 24 is ____

10. Solve the following multiplication and division questions: (6)

a) 11 x 10 = ____

b) 6 x 2 = ____

c) 8 x 5 = ____

d) 77 ÷ 7 = ____

e) 100 ÷ 10 = ____

f) 18 ÷ 3 = ____

11. Write the correct symbol (< > or =) between each group of coins. (3)

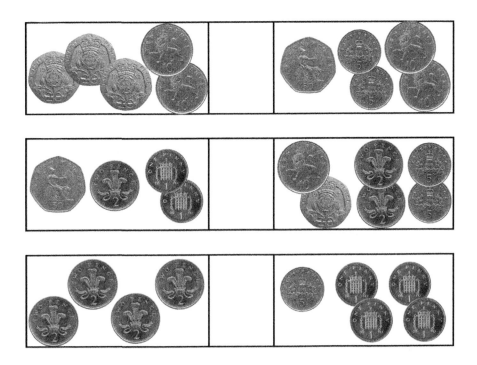

12. Add and subtract 1, 10 and 100 from each of the numbers in the middle of the table below (see example): (9)

-100	-10	-1		+1	+10	+100
0	90	99	*example* 100	101	110	200
			200			
			174			
			421			

13. The shapes below have been rotated in a clockwise direction. Write whether each shape has made a quarter turn, a half turn, a three quarter turn, or a full turn. (4)

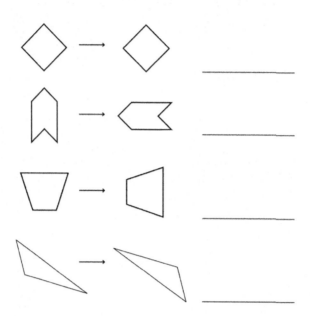

_____

_____

_____

_____

14. Name each of the shapes below and write how many sides each shape has: (8)

Name: _____

Number of sides: _____

Name: _____

Number of sides: _____

Name: _____

Number of sides: _____

Name: _____

Number of sides: _____

Model Answers & Guidance

1. Fill in the missing number sequences below: (2)

+4
<u>140</u>, 144, 148, 152, <u>156</u>, <u>160</u>

-5
80, <u>75</u>, 70, <u>65</u>, 60, <u>55</u>, 50, <u>45</u>

First calculate the size of jump for each sequence – are the numbers increasing or decreasing? By how much? Make sure that each jump is the same size, as sometimes the pattern might involve numbers increasing or decreasing by different increments.

Give one mark for each correct sequence. Deduct one mark for any incorrect responses.

2. Match the additions to the multiplications. One has already been completed for you. (3)

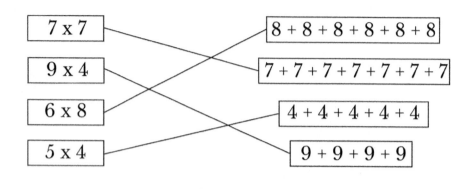

One mark is awarded for each correct answer. These questions are quite simply assessing whether the student understands that multiplication is repeated addition!

3. Place the numbers in the cloud in the correct position so that all the numbers are in order of largest to smallest. (3)

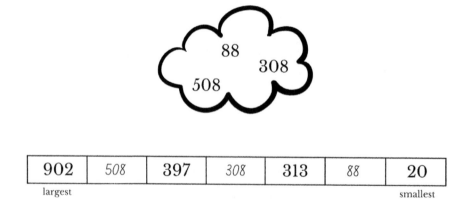

One mark will be awarded for each number that is placed in the correct place. Notice that this question is asking us to order the numbers from largest to smallest — pay attention to this, as sometimes the exam paper will ask us to order the numbers from smallest to largest instead.

Model Answers & Guidance

The examiner is, in short, looking to see how well your child understands place value. Discuss with your child the order in which we look at numbers to be able to compare their sizes — that is, hundreds followed by tens and then the ones. Use these three numbers for the discussion:

341

134

413

All three numbers have the same digits but the biggest number is 413, because it has 4 hundreds; and the smallest number is 132, because it has only 1 hundred.

4. Use each card once to make the smallest total possible. (1)

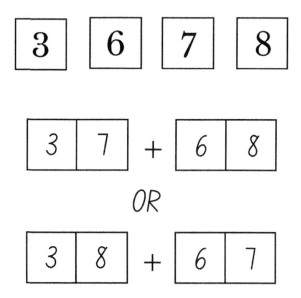

For this question your child should be thinking once again about place value. A key question you could ask to guide them is: *'where should the largest numbers go — in the tens or ones?'*. We would want the smallest numbers (3 and 6) to go in the tens — because 30 and 60 (3 tens and 6 tens) are smaller than 70 and 80 (7 tens and 8 tens).

Award one mark for the correct answer.

5. Work out the following: (4)

    a) 57 - 24 = <u>33</u>

First we look at this question carefully to check whether we can simply take away the tens from one another and then the ones, or if we need to use another method.

Since the number to the left has a bigger ones than the number being taken away from it, this question is straightforward to answer. First we take away the tens from one another (50 - 20 = 30) and then take away the ones from one another (7 - 4 = 3) and add those two answers together (=33).

    b) 85 - 56 = <u>29</u>

Here the examiner is looking to see that your child can do a mental calculation involving two two-digit numbers. One method would be to take 50 away from 85, and then to count back 6 places from 35 to 29.

When it comes to calculations, encourage your child to get into the habit of checking their answers! For this calculation, I would get your child to add together 29 and 56 to check it equals 85.

Alternatively, a student could find the difference, which would involve them counting up from 56 in tens (to 76) and then ones until they get to 85; however, as 85 and 56 are fairly far apart, I would encourage them to use the first method.

Award one mark for each correct answer.

    c) 23 + 75 = <u>98</u>

Simply add together the tens (20 + 70 = 90) and then the ones (3 + 5 = 8). Then add the two totals together (90 + 8 = 98).

Model Answers & Guidance

d) 19 + 69 = <u>88</u>

Once again, mentally add tens and ones separately (10 + 60 = 70 and 9 + 9 = 18) and then add the two totals together (70 + 18 = 88).

6. Amit wants to set the time on his new wristwatch.

His digital clock is showing the time in the picture below.

Draw the hands on the analogue wristwatch below so that it shows the same time. (2)

One mark for the hour hand being in the right position and one mark for the minutes hand. Remember that the student is expected to draw the hour hand slightly beyond 4 — if it is too near 5, however, the student will lose the mark.

7. Buffy the Beaver has a piece of wood.

It is 4 metres and 20 cm in length.

She breaks it into 3 equal pieces.

How long is each piece? (1)

Discuss with the student how many centimetres there are in 4m 20cm (=420cm). The next step is to find out 420 ÷ 3. Now many children in Year 2 would not yet have been taught the bus stop method in school, but this does largely depend on the school.

At any rate, you could start off by talking about their knowledge of the 3 times tables and creating a link there (we know that 21 ÷ 3 = 7 so 42 ÷ 3 will make 14, and 420 ÷ 3 = 140). Next, it would be sensible to demonstrate the bus stop method (if they do not already know it), as shown below:

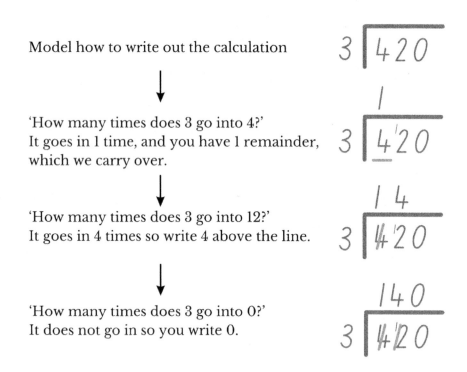

Answer: 1m 40cm

8. Fill in the missing numbers: (3)

a) ¼ of 20 = ½ of <u>10</u>

Model Answers & Guidance

These questions look at your child's understanding of fractions and their ability to link together equivalent fractions. Your child may be able to solve these questions without having to do any calculations, since they will have been introduced to a number of these exact examples when studying fractions in Year 1. Nevertheless, is it still important that they understand how to perform calculations on fractions, so they can proceed with confidence if they get stuck, or if they encounter a more difficult question.

Start by thinking about what a quarter of 20 is – the answer being 5. Now think about what number 5 is half of by doing the inverse and doubling 5 (=10).

Award one mark for each correct answer.

b) ½ of 12 = ¼ of 24

The first step here is for the student to work out what half of 12 is by dividing 12 by the denominator of the fraction, which is 2 (=6). They then need to think of which number 6 is a quarter of, which they can do by simply multiplying 6 by 4 (=24).

c) ⅓ of 15 = ¼ of 20

Start by thinking about what a third of 15 is – the answer being 5. Now think about what number 5 is a quarter of by multiplying 5 by 4 (=20).

9. Fill in the missing numbers: (4)

   a) ½ of 36 is 18

For halving and doubling, your child should continue to use their knowledge of place value, but should also draw on areas they have been taught about earlier in their education – for example, odd and even numbers, as well as division through sharing.

When we halve a number, we divide it by 2. Here your child should first find half of 30 (=15) and then half of 6 (=3), and then add those two figures together (=18).

b) ½ of 44 is 22

We know that 4 divided by 2 = 2. Sure enough, 44 divided by 2 = 22.

c) Double 17 is 34

Back to thinking about tens and ones separately – double the 10 in 17 (=20) then double the 7 (=14), which gives us the answer 34.

d) Double 24 is 48

Once again double the tens (double 20 makes 40) and then double the ones (double 4 equals 8), then add the two answers (40 + 8 = 48).

Award one mark for each correct answer.

10. Solve the following multiplication and division questions: (6)

    a) 11 x 10 = **110**

    b) 6 x 2 = **12**

    c) 8 x 5 = **40**

    d) 77 ÷ 7 = **11**

Model Answers & Guidance

e) $100 \div 10 = \underline{10}$

f) $18 \div 3 = \underline{6}$

These questions simply look to test your child's fluency with the 2, 3, 5, 7 and 10 times tables. These questions should be answered very quickly without the need to calculate.

Award one mark for each correct answer.

11. Write the correct symbol (< > or =) between each group of coins. (3)

Carefully count how many coins there are in each group before determining which side is worth more — or whether the totals are in fact the same!

Award one mark for each correct answer.

12. Add and subtract 1, 10 and 100 from each of the numbers in the middle of the table below (see example): (9)

-100	-10	-1		+1	+10	+100
0	90	99	*example* 100	101	110	200
100	190	199	200	201	210	300
74	164	173	174	175	184	274
321	411	420	421	422	431	521

Caution and care are paramount here: the student needs to make sure they are adding or subtracting from the original number (that is, the number given in the grey boxes in the middle of the table). Students can sometimes get confused and start subtracting or adding from the numbers they are inputting into the table!

Award three marks for each row that has been completed correctly. Deduct one mark if there is one incorrect response within a row. Deduct two marks if a row contains two errors. Award zero marks if a row contains three or more errors.

. . .

Model Answers & Guidance

13. The shapes below have been rotated in a clockwise direction. Write whether each shape has made a quarter turn, a half turn, a three quarter turn, or a full turn. (4)

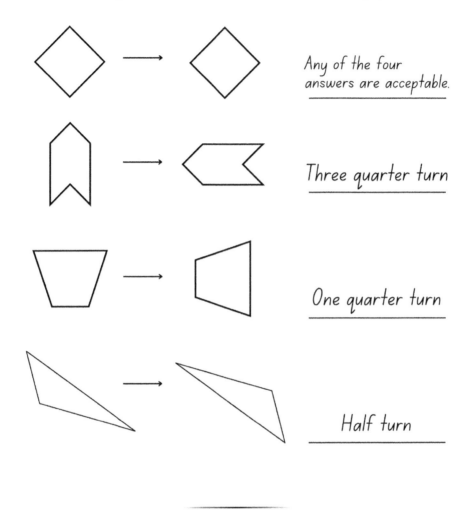

Shape One: you get the same result if you make a quarter turn, a half turn, a three quarters, or a full turn, so accept any of these answers.

Shape Two: The arrow started off facing upwards and is now facing left. Since we are moving in a clockwise direction, this means it has done a three quarter turn (=270 degrees).

Shape Three: This trapezoid has been turned 90 degrees to the right, which makes it a quarter turn.

Shape Four: this triangle's new position is the opposite to where it started, so it has turned half way round (180 degrees).

Award one mark for each correct answer.

14. Name each of the shapes below and write how many sides each shape has: (8)

Name: *Parallelogram*
Number of sides: 4

Name: *Heptagon*
Number of sides: 7

Name: *Oval*
Number of sides: 1

Name: *Trapezium (accept quadrilateral)*
Number of sides: 4

Remember, the sides of a shape are the lines around it.

Award one mark for each shape that has been correctly named, and one mark for each time the correct number of sides has been identified.

Paper Three: The Application Paper

Although the Application Paper is also a relatively brief paper, it is long enough to present candidates with some novel challenges — namely, it requires students to apply their knowledge in unexpected ways. You will also notice a greater emphasis on word problems in this paper! In all, the student has 35 minutes to tackle this paper, and there are 47 marks at stake.

The Application Paper
35 MINUTES: 16 QUESTIONS, 37 MARKS

1. Fill in the missing numbers. (3)

$$2 + \boxed{} = 10$$

$$\boxed{} + 8 = 30$$

$$17 + 7 = \boxed{}$$

2. Calculate the following sums: (2)

$$\begin{array}{r} 18 \\ +\,41 \\ \hline \end{array} \qquad \begin{array}{r} 47 \\ +\,31 \\ \hline \end{array}$$

3. Draw lines between numbers that add together to make 25. This will help Sam the Spider know where to weave his web!

One has been done for you. (4)

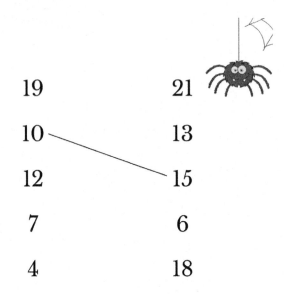

4. Sort the numbers in the number cloud into the correct box along the number line. (2)

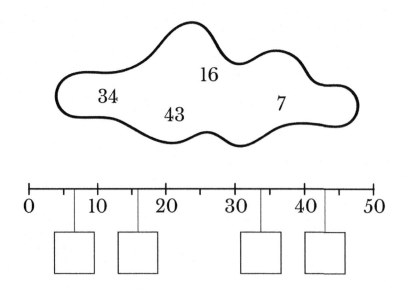

The Application Paper

5. Fill in the blank digits. (1)

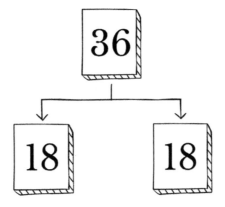

6. Here is one way to partition 36.

Fill in the diagrams below, showing two other ways to partition 36. (3)

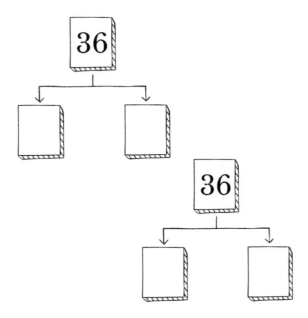

7. There are forty mints in Grandma Lucille's bowl.

Tobias takes 9

Lindsey takes 27.

How many mints are left? (2)

_____ mints

8. First thing in the morning, there are 56 books in the school library.

Before lunch, 13 books are withdrawn from the library.

After lunch, 28 books are returned to the library.

How many books are in the library now? (2)

_____ books

9. Rupert has a collection of Pokemon cards.

He packs them into special storage sleeves.

Each sleeve holds 6 cards.

He fills up 7 sleeves.

How many Pokemon cards does he have in total? (2)

_____ Pokemon cards

10. Circle the shapes that have ⅔ of their area shaded. (2)

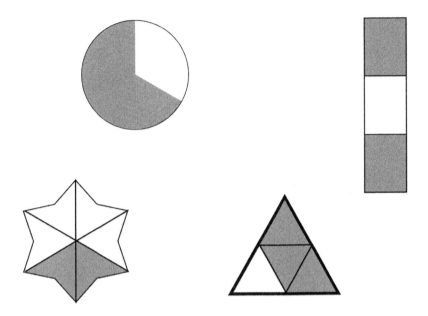

11. Shuai has these three number panels.

He uses them to make 2 digit numbers.

List all of the 2 digit numbers Shuai can make with these panels. (3)

12. Raymon the Robin wants the eggs in his nest to add up to 1,500. Fill in the two blank eggs to help Raymond on his mission! (2)

13. List 3 numbers less than 10 which add up to 25. (2)

_____

14. List these sums of money in size order, beginning with the smallest amount. (2)

£4.77   34p   £8.27

£0.79   £11

☐ ☐ ☐ ☐ ☐
smallest

15. Goneril and Regan are going to a birthday party.

Goneril buys a card that costs 85p

Regan buys a card that costs 20p less.

Circle the coins Regan used. (2)

16. Here are the first three cards in a fantasy card game.

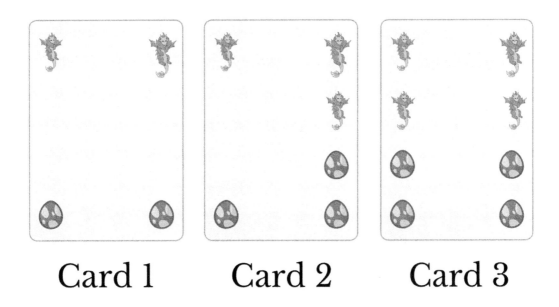

Card 1   Card 2   Card 3

a. How many eggs will be on card number 9? (1)

Answer: _____

b. How many dragons and eggs will there be in total on card number 5? (2)

Answer: _____

Model Answers & Guidance

1. Fill in the missing numbers. (3)

$$2 + \boxed{8} = 10$$

$$\boxed{22} + 8 = 30$$

$$17 + 7 = \boxed{24}$$

TOP: To calculate this, we simply work backwards and subtract 2 from 10, which gives us 8.

MIDDLE: We follow the same method again: we subtract 8 from 30. This gives us 22.

BOTTOM: A fairly straightforward addition question. It may help to break 17 down into one 10 and one 7, and to then add 7 and 7 (=14), before finally adding 14 and 10. At any rate, the answer is 24.

2. Calculate the following sums: (2)

$$\begin{array}{r} 18 \\ +\,41 \\ \hline 59 \end{array} \qquad \begin{array}{r} 47 \\ +\,31 \\ \hline 78 \end{array}$$

This question is testing the student's familiarity with the column method.

Make sure you carefully tally both the units and the tens — it is easy to lose marks here if tackled too hastily.

3. Draw lines between numbers that add together to make 25. This will help Sam the Spider know where to weave his web!

One has been done for you. (4)

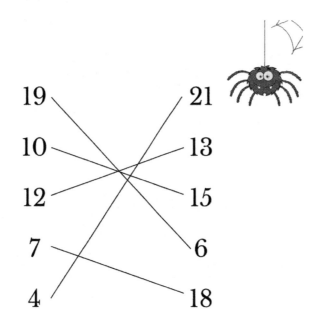

We are pairing numbers here that, when taken together, add up to 25.

The easiest way to approach this is to pick one of the numbers on the left-hand side - for instance, 19 - and subtract it from 25.

25 - 19 = 6.

As a result, we draw a line from 19 to 6.

Then we simply repeat this process with the other numbers on the left-hand side. Subtract the number in question from 25. The number you are left will tell you where to draw the line.

4. Sort the numbers in the number cloud into the correct box along the number line. (2)

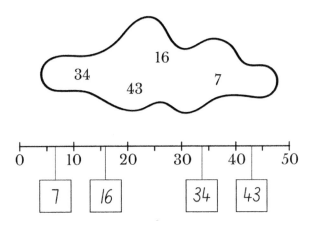

We are, in effect, being asked to order the numbers in the cloud from smallest to largest. However, the numbers already on the 'number line' makes our life a little bit easier. After all, we know that 7, for instance, must fall between 0 and 10, and that 34 must fall between 30 and 40.

Make sure you are using the numbers already on the 'number line' to check your work.

5. Fill in the blank digits. (1)

$$\boxed{6}\,\boxed{3} + \boxed{3}\,\boxed{7} = \boxed{1}\,\boxed{0}\,\boxed{0}$$

Here is a good way of looking at this question.

We are being asked to work out which two numbers add up to make 100.

We know that one of the two numbers contains six 10s. And that the other contains seven 1s. In total, that tallies up to 67.

If we minus these tens and units from 100 we get the following:

100 - 67 = 33.

So we know that we need three more 10s, and three more 1s.

So we put a '3' in the units box, to the right-hand side of the 6. And we put another '3' in the tens box, to the left-hand side of the 7.

6. Here is one way to partition 36.

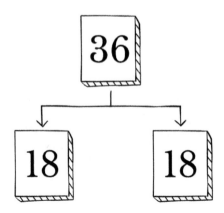

Fill in the diagrams below, showing two other ways to partition 36. (3)

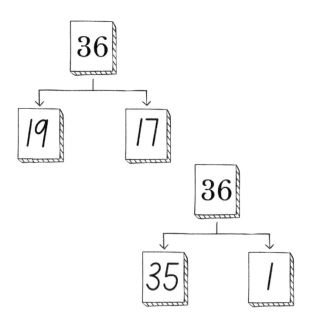

The student needs to offer two separate pairings that add up to 36 (and must not use 18 and 18, which was used in the example).

Above, I have given two possible answers. However, any other valid answer will also be credited.

7. There are forty mints in Grandma Lucille's bowl.

Tobias takes 9

Lindsey takes 27.

How many mints are left? (2)

$$9 + 27 = 36$$

$$40 - 36 = 4$$

For word problems, it is useful if you get your child to really try and visualise what is happening.

This is a two-step problem. The student may decide to first add together all the mints that Tobias and Lindsey have taken (9 + 27 = 36) and then take that total away from the 40 mints in the bowl (40 - 36 = 4). Or, they could take away the mints in steps. Either way, award two marks for the correct answers, and one if their method was correct but the answer was incorrect.

Answer: 4 mints

8. First thing in the morning, there are 56 books in the school library.

Before lunch, 13 books are withdrawn from the library.

After lunch, 28 books are returned to the library.

How many books are in the library now? (2)

Model Answers & Guidance

$$56 - 13 = 43$$

$$43 + 28 = 71$$

In this case the school library start off with 56 books and by lunchtime they lend out 13 books, so we start off by writing 56 - 13 = 43. So the library now has 43 books. But then 28 are returned after lunch (43 + 28 = 71), which means the library ends up with 71 books.

Award two marks for the correct answer and deduct a mark if the answer is incorrect but the method is correct (in other words, if they simply did not add up 6 and 15 correctly).

Answer: 71 books

9. Rupert has a collection of Pokemon cards.

He packs them into special storage sleeves.

Each sleeve holds 6 cards.

He fills up 7 sleeves.

How many Pokemon cards does he have in total? (2)

Your child may read this problem and be able to identify that they need to write 6 x 7 = 42 or they may choose to draw their working out before writing the numerical answer. Whichever method they choose is fine, since both shows they understand the demands of the question. Award two marks for the correct answer and one if the method is correct but the answer is incorrect.

Answer: <u>42 Pokemon cards</u>

10. Circle the shapes that have ⅔ of their area shaded. (2)

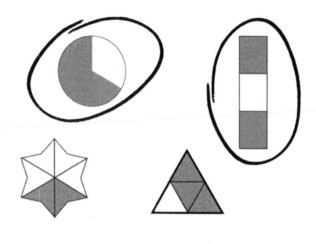

One mark for each correct answer. Recap that ⅔ means two parts out of three.

The top left and top right shape are divided into three parts, of which two parts are shaded. So it is easy to see that both of them have been ⅔ shaded.

The bottom left shape is a bit trickier, as it has been broken into six equal parts. We need to be able to see that four of these parts would need to be shaded in order for the shape to be ⅔ all in all. However, since only two parts out of six are shaded, we know that it is in fact just ⅓ shaded.

The bottom right shape has been broken into four equal shapes, of which three have been shaded. This means that it is ¾, *not* ⅔ shaded.

11. Shuai has these three number panels.

He uses them to make 2 digit numbers.

List all of the 2 digit numbers Shuai can make with these panels. (3)

We are being asked to make as many 2 digit numbers as possible from the three numbers provided.

A good method is to pick one of the three number to be used in the 'tens' column, and see what numbers we can make — and then to repeat the process with the other two numbers. This gives us:

Answer: 38; 35; 83; 85; 53; 58.

12. Raymon the Robin wants the eggs in his nest to add up to 1,500. Fill in the two blank eggs to help Raymond on his mission! (2)

The first task is to subtract the three numbers already featured in the nest from 1,500.

One way of doing this is to add the three numbers up, and then to subtract their total from 1,500.

700 + 500 + 50 = 1,250

1,500 - 1,250 = 250

This tells us that the numbers we put into each of the two blank eggs need to add up to 250.

We can then use any two numbers that add up to 250. Above, I have used 200 and 50 — but any two numbers that sum up to 250 will be credited.

13. List 3 different numbers less than 10 which add up to 23. (2)

Model Answers & Guidance

One method of tackling this is to add together the two largest numbers under 10 (9 and 8), and then to see how much more you need to add in order to reach 23.

9 + 8 = 17

Therefore, since 23 - 17 = 6, we know that we need 6 more to reach 23.

As a result, the correct answer is 9, 8 and 6.

Answer: 9, 8, 6

14. List these sums of money in size order, beginning with the smallest amount. (2)

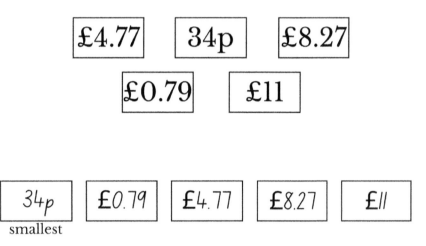

It's important to work carefully when dealing with questions that ask us to order numbers (or in this case money) in either increasing or decreasing order.

Also, keep in mind that 34p is identical to £0.34. As a result, it is the smaller amount of the five we have been presented with — *not* the biggest.

15. Goneril and Regan are going to a birthday party.

Goneril buys a card that costs 85p

Regan buys a card that costs 20p less.

Circle the coins Regan used. (2)

This question is split into two parts. Firstly, the student needs to recognise that Regan's card cost 65p (20p less than than Goneril's). Next they need to circle a group of coins that will equal 65p. Two points will be awarded if they chose any of the two coin combinations shown below.

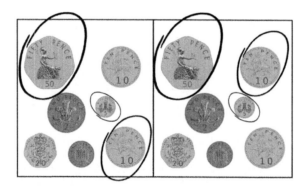

16. Here are the first three cards in a fantasy card game.

Model Answers & Guidance

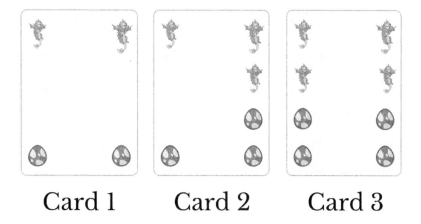

Card 1   Card 2   Card 3

a. How many eggs will be on card number 9? (1)

Card 1 has two eggs; Card 2 has three eggs; and Card 3 has four eggs.

The pattern is clear: to deduce the number of eggs you will find on a certain card, you simply take the card number and add one. As a result, we can infer that Card 9 will have ten eggs.

Answer: 10 eggs.

b. How many dragons and eggs will there be in total on card number 5? (2)

On every card, the number of dragons present is always exactly equal to the number of eggs present.

Using the logic we used in the previous question, we know that there will be 6 eggs on card number 5 — and therefore we know also that there will be 6 dragons on card 5 as well.

So we simply need to do 6 + 6 (=12) to find our answer.

Answer: 12

Paper Four: The Number and Calculation Paper

Although this paper covers a broad range of topics, it focuses on number and calculation to a greater degree than any other sub-topic. We see this in its penchant for arithmetic questions, but also for word problems, which require students to figure out whether to add, subtract, multiply or divide based on certain key words.

Unlike the previous papers so far, this paper also assesses your child on symmetry as well as positions and directions.

This paper consists of 21 questions, for which students are allocated 40 minutes. Time is thus tighter on this paper than in the ones previously encountered in this guide, so it is important to move through the questions with speed — particularly the arithmetic questions.

The Number and Calculation Paper

40 MINUTES: 21 QUESTION, 57 MARKS

1. Calculate the following: (9)

a) 8 + 5 = ____

b) 18 - 9 = ____

c) 9 x 2 = ____

d) 42 ÷ 6 = ____

e) 14 + 6 = ____

f) 38 ÷ 2 = ____

g) 9 x 7 = ____

h) 170 ÷ 10 = ____

i) 46 + 37 = ____

2. Fill in the blanks: (6)

a) ____ ÷ 3 = 8

b) ____ - 8 = 23

c) 34 - ____ = 18

d) 36 ÷ ____ = 6

e) 24 + 4 = 30 - ____

f) 19 + ____ + 11 = 41

3. Luigi has 54 fossils.

He gives 9 of them to his friend.

How many fossils does Luigi have left? (1)

Answer: _____

4. A can of lemonade costs 25 pence.

How much do 8 cans of lemonade cost? (1)

Answer: _____

5. Coach Steven has 60 football stickers.

He shares them out equally between the 10 children who attend his football club.

How many stickers does each child get? (1)

Answer: _____

6. Melissa can run around the netball court 50 seconds faster than Joanna.

It takes Joanna 140 seconds to run around the netball court.

How long does it take Melissa to run around the court? (1)

_____ seconds

7. Sarah has 11 arcade tokens.

Louisa has 27 more tokens than Sarah.

a) How many tokens does Louisa have? (1)

Answer: _____

b) If Sarah and Louisa put their tokens together to buy a prize, how many tokens would they have? (1)

Answer: _____

c) A kite costs 43 tokens.

How many tokens would they have left if they bought a kite? (1)

Answer: _____

d) How many tokens would four kites cost? (1)

Answer: _____

8. 51 Americans want to take a tour of London.

Each minivan can transport a maximum of 7 tourists.

How many minivans are needed to take all the tourists on a tour at once? (1)

Answer: _____

9. Esme has 32p and James has half as much money as Esme.

How much money do Esme and James have in total? (2)

Answer: _____

10. Janet lives 45 minutes from the supermarket.

She leaves her home at 9.15 to go shopping.

What time does she get to the supermarket? (1)

Answer: _____

11. Which two numbers are added together to make 100? Fill in the boxes below. (1)

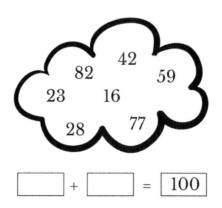

12. Use these three numbers to create four <u>different</u> facts: (3)

3   27   9

3 × 9 = 27

9 × ☐ = ☐

☐ ÷ ☐ = 9

☐ ÷ 9 = ☐

13. Put the correct signs (+, -, x, ÷) in the blank boxes. (2)

42 ☐ 42 = 84

54 ☐ 29 = 25

5 ☐ 8 = 40

25 ☐ 5 = 5

14. Circle the coins you would use to make 83p. (1)

15. Continue the number patterns below. (3)

2, 7, 12, 17, 22, ___, ___

7, 16, 25, 34, 43, ___, ___

37, 31, 25, 19, 13, ___, ___

16. Write the time below each clock. (2)

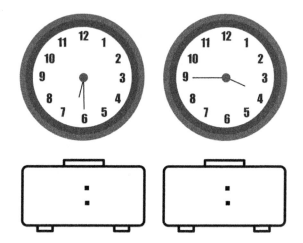

17. Round each number to the nearest 10. (4)

35 _____

44 _____

56 _____

98 _____

18. Take a look at the triangle to the right. (4)

a) What fraction of this triangle is shaded?

Answer:_____

b) What fraction of this triangle has a shape in it?

Answer:_____

c) What fraction of this triangle has a square in it?

Answer:_____

d) What fraction is unshaded and has a heart in it?

Answer:_____

19. Fill in the magic square below using the numbers 1 to 9. You can only use each number once and you need to make sure each line adds up to 15. (2)

		2
1	5	
8		4

20. On the shapes below, draw a straight line through the dot. The line you add should cut the shape into two equal halves. (6)

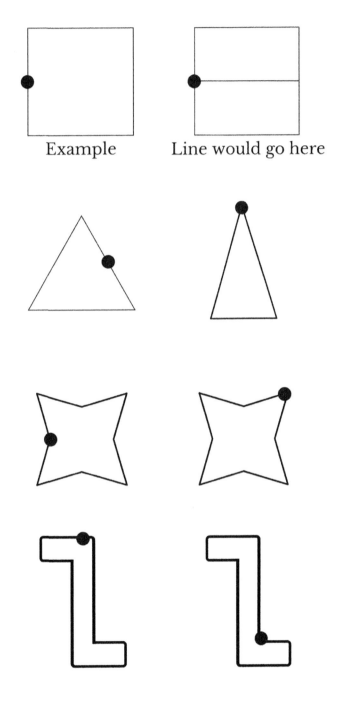

21. Complete the instructions to help guide the mouse to the cheese. (2)

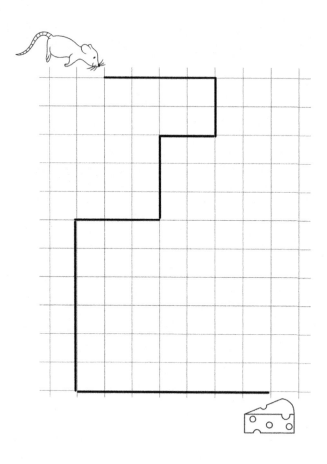

RIGHT 4 SQUARES

DOWN 2 SQUARES

_____

_____

_____

_____

_____

Model Answers & Guidance

1. Calculate the following: (9)

a) 8 + 5 = <u>13</u>

Your child can use their knowledge of doubles to solve this. We know 5 + 5 = 10; as a result, we know that 8 + 5 will be 3 more than this, and thus 13.

b) 18 - 9 = <u>9</u>

For this question you can get your child to think about taking away 10 from 18 and then adding 1 back on at the end. Alternatively, they can count the difference between 9 and 18.

c) 9 x 2 = <u>18</u>

This question looks at your child's ability to recount their 2 times tables.

d) 42 ÷ 6 = <u>7</u>

This question looks at your child's ability to recount their 6 times tables and corresponding division facts.

e) 14 + 6 = <u>20</u>

This question is looking to see if your child is able to recall number bonds for 20.

f) 38 ÷ 2 = <u>19</u>

Here your child needs to think about halving 3 tens (which gives us 15) and 8 ones (which gives us 4) to get 19 as the final answer.

g) 9 x 7 = <u>63</u>

This question looks at your child's ability to recount their 7 times tables.

h) 170 ÷ 10 = <u>17</u>

When we divide a number by 10, we move all of its digits one place to the right in a place value grid. So when we divide 170 by 10, 1 hundred becomes 1 ten, and 7 tens become 7 ones. The image to the right demonstrates this process in action!

thousands	hundreds	tens	ones (units) •	tenths	hundredths
	1	7	0		
		1	7		

One mark is awarded for each correct answer.

i) 46 + 37 = <u>83</u>

Encourage your child to mentally add the tens then the ones. Alternatively, they could take 3 away from 46 and give it to the 37, so that the question becomes 43 + 40, which may be easier for students to tackle.

2. Fill in the blanks: (6)

a) <u>24</u> ÷ 3 = 8

Here you need to multiply in order to find the missing number as the dividend is missing. So 8 x 3 = 24, which means 24 is the missing number.

b) <u>31</u> - 8 = 23

When given a missing number subtraction question with the first number missing, you need to do the inverse (opposite) operation. So 23 + 8 = 31 which means the missing number is 31.

    c) 34 - <u>16</u> = 18

When you are missing the middle number in a subtraction question, you need to subtract the last number from the first number to find the answer.

    d) 36 ÷ <u>6</u> = 6

When you are missing the middle number in a division question, you need to divide the first number by the last number to find the answer.

    e) 24 + 4 = 30 - <u>2</u>

This question requires your child to balance out the calculation. First add 24 and 4 (=28) to work out what the other (missing) side needs to equal. Then take away 28 from 30 to find the missing number (=2).

    f) 19 + <u>11</u> + 11 = 41

Model Answers & Guidance

Add together 11 and 19 (=30), then take that total away from 41 to find the missing number (41 - 30 = 11).

3. Luigi has 54 fossils.

He gives 9 of them to his friend.

How many fossils does Luigi have left? (1)

54 − 9 = 45

45 fossils

The key word that tells us we need to subtract is the word 'left' at the end of the question.

One mark for the correct calculation and answer.

Answer: 45 fossils

4. A can of lemonade costs 25 pence.

How much do 8 cans of lemonade cost? (1)

25p x 8 = 200p or £2.00

£2.00 or 200p

We know how much one can of lemonade costs; so to find how much 8 would cost, we need to multiply. A mark would be awarded for the correct calculation and answer (in either pence or pounds).

Answer: £2.00 or 200p

5. Coach Steven has 60 football stickers.

He shares them out equally between the 10 children who attend his football club.

How many stickers does each child get? (1)

$60 \div 10 = 6$

6 stickers each

We know we need to divide because we are told the football stickers need to be 'shared out equally'.

One mark for the correct calculation and answer.

Answer: 6 stickers each

6. Melissa can run around the netball court 50 seconds faster than Joanna.

It takes Joanna 140 seconds to run around the netball court.

How long does it take Melissa to run around the court? (1)

140 seconds − 50 seconds = 90 seconds

<u>90</u> seconds

Melissa is faster than Joanna, and thus her track time will be smaller than Joanna's — as a result, this means we have to subtract from Joanna's time to find our answer.

One mark for the correct calculation and answer.

Answer: <u>90 seconds</u>

7. Sarah has 11 arcade tokens.

Louisa has 27 more tokens than Sarah.

a) How many tokens does Louisa have? (1)

11 + 27 = 38

<u>38</u> tokens

The word 'more' tells us we need to add the 27 to the 11 Sarah has in order to find out how many tokens Louisa has.

One mark for answering the question correctly.

Answer: 38 tokens

b) If Sarah and Louisa put their tokens together to buy a prize, how many tokens would they have? (1)

11 + 38 = 49

49 tokens

The key here to remember that we are now adding the total from the first question to the amount of tokens Sarah has.

One mark for correctly answering this part of the question.

Answer: 49 tokens

c) A kite costs 43 tokens.

How many tokens would they have left if they bought a kite? (1)

49 - 43 = 6

6 tokens

The word 'left' tells us this is a subtraction question; and because it asks how much 'they' would have left, we need to subtract the cost of the kite from their joint total (49 tokens).

Award one mark for the correct answer.

Answer: <u>6 tokens</u>

d) How many tokens would four kites cost? (1)

4 x 43 tokens = 172

<u>172</u> tokens

Some 7+ Maths papers can really stretch a candidate's comprehension skills. This whole question is a good example of this. In the last two parts of this question, the child needs to refer back to information gleaned from previous parts of the question. Here, they need to carry forward the fact that one kite is 43 tokens; so to find how much 4 kites would cost, we need to multiply by 4.

Award one mark for the correct answer.

Answer: <u>172 tokens</u>

8. 51 Americans want to take a tour of London.

Each minivan can transport a maximum of 7 tourists.

How many minivans are needed to take all the tourists on a tour at once? (1)

7 + 7 + 7 + 7 + 7 + 7 + 7 = 49 or 7 x 7 = 49

<u>8</u> minivans

For this question, your child needs to use their knowledge of the 7 times tables/skip counting in sevens. Once they work out that seven sevens is 49 they will realise they need eight minivan to fit in the final two (50th and 51st) people.

One mark for reaching the answer '8'. The method used and recorded for working out the answer is up to the individual.

Answer: 8 minivans

9. Esme has 32p and James has half as much money as Esme. How much money do Esme and James have in total? (2)

$32 \div 2 = 16$

$16 + 32 = 48$

48p

This is a two-part question. First we need to find out how much money James has — we are told it is half of the amount Esme has. We know that, when we halve, we divide by 2. Then we are given the phrase ' in total', which tells us we need to add the amount of money each child has.

Award two marks for the correct answer — and one mark if parts of the calculation are correct, yet the final answer is incorrect.

Answer: 48p

10. Janet lives 45 minutes from the supermarket. She leaves her home at 9.15 to go shopping.

Model Answers & Guidance

What time does she get to the supermarket? (1)

10:00

Encourage your child to visualise where the clock hands will be at 9:15am. Discuss how 45 minutes is three quarters of an hour and therefore a three-quarters turn. Use this to visualise how the minute hand will end up at 12, while the hour hand will move from slightly after 9 to exactly on 10.

One mark for writing 10:00.

Answer: 10:00

11. Which two numbers are added together to make 100? Fill in the boxes below. (1)

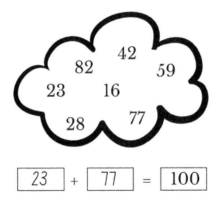

Encourage your child to think about their number bonds to 10 and then 100. Once they realise the pair they are looking for has a 3 and a 7 in the units/ones, then they can narrow down the pair they are looking for.

One mark for choosing the correct pair of numbers.

12. Use these three numbers to create four <u>different</u> facts: (3)

3   27   9

$$\boxed{3} \times \boxed{9} = \boxed{27}$$

$$\boxed{9} \times \boxed{3} = \boxed{27}$$

$$\boxed{27} \div \boxed{3} = \boxed{9}$$

$$\boxed{27} \div \boxed{9} = \boxed{3}$$

Award one mark for each correct calculation. Each calculation must be different, so ensure the two division ones are not the same.

13. Put the correct signs (+, -, x, ÷) in the blank boxes. (2)

$$42 \boxed{+} 42 = 84$$

$$54 \boxed{-} 29 = 25$$

$$5 \boxed{\times} 8 = 40$$

$$25 \boxed{\div} 5 = 5$$

Model Answers & Guidance

For each question, encourage the student to look at where the biggest number is, as this will help them work out whether they need to multiply/add or divide/subtract. Award 2 marks for all the signs being in the correct place. Take away one mark for any incorrect answers.

14. Circle the coins you would use to make 83p. (1)

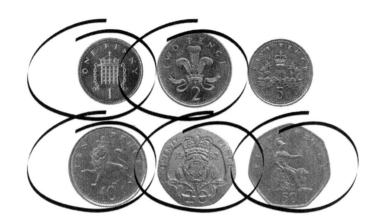

Award one mark for circling all the coins besides the 5p coin.

15. Continue the number patterns below. (3)

2, 7, 12, 17, 22, _27_, _32_

7, 16, 25, 34, 43, _52_, _61_

37, 31, 25, 19, 13, _7_, _1_

First calculate the size of jump for each sequence – are the numbers increasing or decreasing? By how much? Make sure that each jump is the same size, as sometimes the pattern might involve numbers increasing or decreasing by different increments.

Give one mark for each correct sequence. Deduct one mark for any incorrect responses.

16. Write the time below each clock. (2)

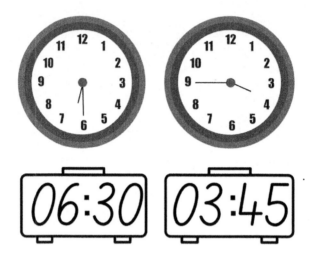

Accept answers in 12 hour or 24 hour form — for instance, either 06:30 *or* 18:30 is an acceptable answer for the left-hand clock.

One mark for each correct answer.

17. Round each number to the nearest 10. (4)

35   40

44   40

56   60

98   100

Model Answers & Guidance

Recap the rounding rules with your child. If the number ends in five or above, you round up to the next 10; if it is 4 or below, you round down.

Award one mark for each correct answer.

18. Take a look at the triangle to the right. (4)

a) What fraction of this triangle is shaded?

³/₄

This question is pretty straightforward as it is clear the triangle is divided into four parts and three parts out of those four has been shaded.

Answer: ³/₄

b) What fraction of this triangle has a shape in it?

³/₄

Only one quarter of the triangle — to the bottom left — does not have a shape in it. As a result, the correct answer is again ³/₄.

Answer: ³/₄

c) What fraction of this triangle has a square in it?

¹/₄

Only one of the quarter segments contains a square. As such, we can assert with confidence that ¼ of the triangle contains a square.

Answer: ¼

d) What fraction is unshaded and has a heart in it?

¹/₄

Only one of the quarter segments is unshaded, and this segment also contains a heart. So the correct answer is ¼.

Answer: ¼

19. Fill in the magic square below using the numbers 1 to 9. You can only use each number once and you need to make sure each line adds up to 15. (2)

6	7	2
1	5	9
8	3	4

The key is to start with the empty box on the right hand side in the middle row. We need to find a number that would work with 1 + 5 and 2 + 4 to make 15. Once we establish that 9 goes there, we move on to either 8 and 4 on the bottom row, or 1 and 8 in the left column. Once you have those two filled in, you complete the magic square by writing '7' in the middle place on the top row.

Award two marks if all the numbers are in the correct position and one if any of the numbers are incorrect.

20. On the shapes below, draw a straight line through the dot.

The line you add should cut the shape into two equal halves. (6)

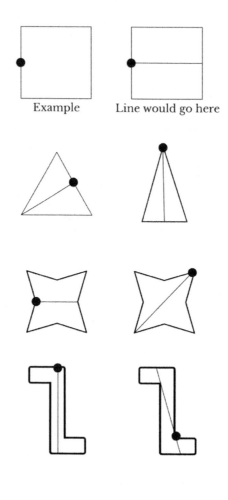

You will often see questions in 7+ papers that ask you to draw a line of symmetry on a shape.

This question is similar, yet does differ slightly. The lines I have drawn through the top four shapes (excluding the exemplar) not only split the shapes into two equal halves; they also function as lines of symmetry. Both sides are symmetrical to one another.

However, while the lines drawn through the bottom two shapes do split them into two equal parts, they are not lines of symmetry.

Model Answers & Guidance

Encourage students to pay attention to whether they are being asked to draw a line of symmetry, or whether they are simply being asked to slice a shape into halves.

Award a mark for each shape.

21. Complete the instructions to help guide the mouse to the cheese. (2)

RIGHT 4

DOWN 2

Left 2

Down 3

Left 3

Down 6

Right 7

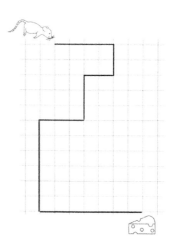

Two marks for writing all the instructions correctly. Deduct one mark for one error, and two marks for two errors.

Paper Five: The Incremental Calculation Paper

In the Incremental Calculation Paper, we find questions that increase in difficulty as the paper progresses — and this especially applies to questions that exercise candidates' calculation skills.

Nevertheless, this paper covers most of the topics children will have covered in school — number, calculation, time, measurements, money, fractions and word problems. Indeed, the one area not covered in this paper is shapes, though this area is covered amply in other papers within this guide.

Your child has 45 minutes to answer all the questions, and there are 57 marks at stake.

The Incremental Calculation Paper
45 MINUTES: 47 QUESTIONS; 57 MARKS

1. What is the value of the 5 in the number 52? (1)

Answer: _____

2. Order the numbers below from smallest to largest: (2)

693

72

432

89

_____

3. Write the number 567 in words. (1)

_____

Solve the following calculations by filling in the blanks: (9)

4.

    4 + ____ = 10

5.

    7 + ____ = 10

6.

    7 + 9 = ____

7.

    16 + 8 = ____

8.

    28 + 77 = ____

9.

    ____ + 7 = 24

10.

    45 - 9 = ____

11.

    97 - 34 = ____

12.

    77 - ____ = 39

Balance the calculations by filling in the blanks: (3)

13.

    13 + ____ = 18 + 7

14.

    38 - ____ = 17 + 9

15.

    65 = 26 + 33 + ____

Solve the following calculations: (5)

16.

    8 x 2 = ____

17.

    9 x 5 = ____

18.

    310 ÷ 10 = ____

19.

$95 \div 5 = \underline{}$

20.

$92 \div 2 = \underline{}$

Solve the following calculations by filling in the blanks: (2)

21.

$72 \div \underline{} = 12$

22.

$\underline{} \div 7 = 3$

Continue the number patterns below: (5)

23.

19   21   23   25   ____

24.

25   29   33   37   ____

25.

7   8   10   13   ____

26.

    240   120   60   30   ____

27.

    62   60   56   48   ____   0

28. Hilary has 17 marbles and Joseph has 15. How many marbles do they have all in all? (1)

                                                      Answer: _____

29. Tariq has 9 fewer Pokemon cards than Weisang.

If Weisang has 35 Pokemon cards, how many does Tariq have? (1)

                                                      Answer: _____

30. Meera has 56 cookies.

She decides to share them out equally between herself and seven friends.

How many cookies do they each get. (1)

                                                      Answer: _____

31. There are 12 lockers in the school's hallway. Each locker contains 8 books. How many books are there in total? (1)

Answer: _____

32. Shade ¾ of the following shape: (1)

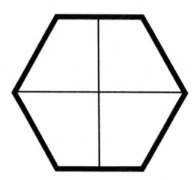

33. The shape below has been divided into 4 equal sections.

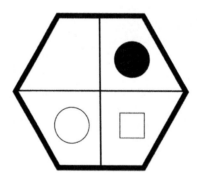

a) What fraction of the shape has a square in it? (1)

Answer: _____

b) What fraction of the shape has a black circle in it? (1)

Answer: _____

c) What fraction does not have a shape in it? (1)

Answer: _____

34. Sagar has 24 chocolates. He gives a quarter of them to his cousin.

How many chocolates does he have remaining for himself? (1)

Answer: _____

35. Rajiv has £3.40 in his wallet and Ralph has 90p in his. How much money do they have in total? (1)

Answer: _____

36. Pierre buys a croissant that costs £3.30. He pays with a £5 note. How much change does he receive? (1)

Answer: _____

37. Esther has £9.60 in her wallet. A bagel costs 90p. If she buys two bagels how much money will she have left? (2)

Answer: _____

38. Round the following numbers to the nearest 10. (2)

a) 25 _____

b) 79 _____

39. Convert the following measurements: (2)

a) 2 ½ litres ____ millilitres

b) 3.5 metres ____ centimetres.

40. Underline the measurement that is closest in length to a bathtub: (1)

92m

12cm

1 ½ metres

300cm

41. Read the analogue clocks and write the time in digital form. (2)

42. Convert the following periods of time: (2)

    a) 3 days   _____ hours

    b) ¾ of an hour   _____ minutes

43. Zach lives a 30 minute walk away from school. If he needs to be there by 8.30am, what time does he need to leave his house? (1)

                                                            Answer: _____

44. Study the image below. Work out the rule and fill in the 3 missing numbers. (2)

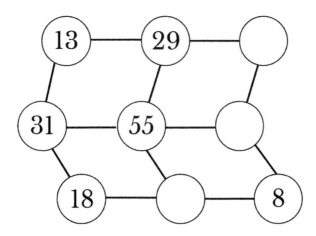

45. Joshua has 6 different coins and each one is worth less than £1. What is the difference between the biggest and the smallest total she could have? (2)

                                                             Answer: _____

46. **Write the letter of the box that comes fifth in the sequence?**
(1)

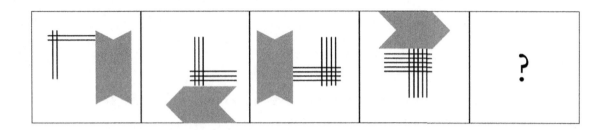

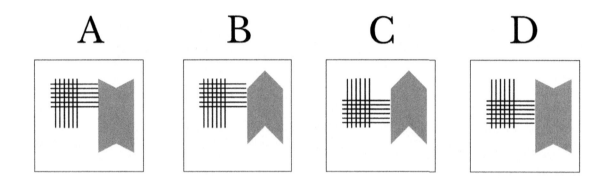

Answer: _____

47. Write the letter of the little box that finishes off the pattern in the big box. (1)

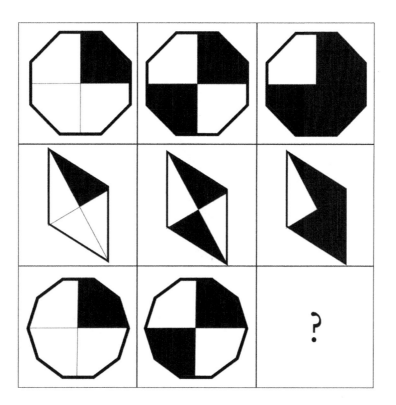

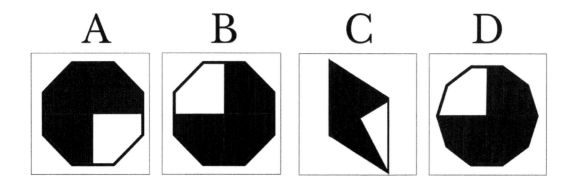

Answer: _____

Model Answers & Guidance

1. What is the value of the 5 in the number 52? (1)

Five tens.

Award one mark for the correct answer.

Answer: <u>Five tens or 50</u>

2. Order the numbers below from smallest to largest: (2)

693

72

432

89

---

72   89   432   693

Encourage your child to look at the place value of each number.

Award two marks for all the numbers being in the correct position. Award one mark if there is just one mistake.

3. Write the number 567 in words. (1)

five hundred and sixty seven

Award one mark for the correct answer and no marks if any parts are spelt incorrectly.

Solve the following calculations by filling in the blanks: (9)

4.

    4 + <u>6</u> = 10

5.

    7 + <u>3</u> = 10

6.

    7 + 9 = <u>16</u>

Encourage your child to add 10 to 7 and then take 1 away from the answer.

. . .

Model Answers & Guidance

7.

16 + 8 = <u>24</u>

8.

28 + 77 = <u>105</u>

It is easier to add multiples of 10 than it is to add 28 so I would encourage your child to add 30 to 77 and then take 2 away from their answer.

9.

<u>17</u> + 7 = 24

To find the answer to this question, your child could do the inverse operation and subtract 7 from 24.

10.

45 - 9 = <u>36</u>

11.

97 - 34 = <u>63</u>

12.

77 - <u>38</u> = 39

Subtract 39 from 77 to find the missing number. Alternatively, count the difference from 39 to 77 (39 add **30** to get to 69; add **8** to get to 77 (30 + 8 = 38)).

Award one mark for each correct answer.

Balance the calculations by filling in the blanks: (3)

13.

13 + <u>12</u> = 18 + 7

Work out what 18 + 7 equals (=25); then calculate what you would need to add to 13 to make 25.

14.

38 - <u>12</u> = 17 + 9

First add 17 and 9 (=26); then work out what you need to take away from 38 to make 26 (=12).

15.

65 = 26 + 33 + <u>6</u>

First add together 26 and 33 (=59), then subtract 59 from 65 to find the missing number.

Award one mark for each correct answer.

Solve the following calculations: (5)

16.

   8 x 2 = 16

17.

   9 x 5 = 45

18.

   310 ÷ 10 = 31

If your child struggles with this question, do some work on place value and exploring what happens to numbers when you either multiply or divide by 10 – namely, how they move left or right on a place value grid.

19.

   95 ÷ 5 = 19

20.

   92 ÷ 2 = 46

Dividing by 2 is the same as halving, so get your child to think about what half of 90 is (=45) and then what half of 2 is (=1). Then ask them to add the two answers together.

Solve the following calculations by filling in the blanks: (2)

21.

72 ÷ <u>6</u> = 12

For this question, your child must divide 72 by 12 to find the missing number.

22.

<u>21</u> ÷ 7 = 3

Remember, when we are given a division question with the first part missing, we need to do the inverse operation to find the answer (7 x 3).

Continue the number patterns below: (5)

23.

19   21   23   25   <u>27</u>

Your child needs to first check the size of the 'jumps' by finding the difference between the first number and the next one (=2) – they should then make sure the jumps are the same throughout the sequence. Once it

Model Answers & Guidance

has been established they are the same, work out what the next number will be after 25.

24.

25   29   33   37   <u>41</u>

Award one mark for correctly identifying the next number in the sequence.

25.

7   8   10   13   <u>17</u>

This is a more challenging sequence as the numbers are going up by a different amount each time. It is critical the student writes out the 'jump' sizes for each 'jump' so they can establish that the amount is different and so they can ascertain the pattern – namely, that each jump is half the size of the jump before it.

$$\overset{+1\ \ +2\ \ +3\ \ +4}{7, 8, 10, 13, \underline{17}}$$

Award one mark for answering this question correctly.

26.

240   120   60   30   <u>15</u>

$$\overset{-120}{\curvearrowright}\ \overset{-60}{\curvearrowright}\ \overset{-30}{\curvearrowright}\ \overset{-15}{\curvearrowright}$$
$$240,\ 120,\ 60,\ 30,\ \underline{15}$$

Once again we are given a question where the 'jumps' are different, but this time we are subtracting (not adding) by an increasing amount each time — indeed, the amount we are subtracting by halves with each number in the sequence.

27.

62   60   56   48   <u>32</u>   0

$$\overset{-2}{\curvearrowright}\ \overset{-4}{\curvearrowright}\ \overset{-8}{\curvearrowright}\ \overset{-16}{\curvearrowright}\ \overset{-32}{\curvearrowright}$$
$$62,\ 60,\ 56,\ 48,\ \underline{32},\ 0$$

This question requires your child to notice the numbers in the sequences are decreasing and that each 'jump' goes down by double the 'jump' before.

28. Hilary has 17 marbles and Joseph has 15. How many marbles do they have all in all? (1)

$$17 + 15 = 32$$

<u>32 marbles</u>

Model Answers & Guidance

The key phrase here is 'all in all' which tells us we need to add the two amounts we are given in the word problem.

Award one mark for the correct answer.

Answer: <u>32 Marbles</u>

29. Tariq has 9 fewer Pokemon cards than Weisang.

If Weisang has 35 Pokemon cards, how many does Tariq have? (1)

$$35 - 9 = 26$$

<u>26</u> Pokemon cards

The key word here is 'fewer' which tells us we need to take away 9 from 35 to find the answer.

Award one mark for the correct answer.

Answer: <u>26 Pokemon Cards</u>

30. Meera has 56 cookies.

She decides to share them out equally between herself and <u>seven friends.</u>

How many cookies do they each get. (1)

<u>7</u> cookies

The key word that lets us know we need to divide is the word 'share'. The words '…herself and her friends' is underlined to make it clear that the 56 cookies have to be divided up/shared between 8 people. The student might choose to draw out the problem.

Award one mark for the correct answer.

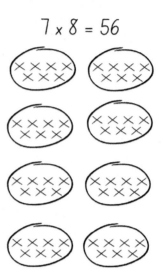

Answer: 7 Cookies

31. There are 12 lockers in the school's hallway. Each locker contains 8 books. How many books are there in total? (1)

<u>96</u> books

Your child may decide to draw an array to find the answer to this question. If they find multiplication questions like these difficult, get them to draw pictures and really visualise the problem.

Award one mark for the correct answer.

$8 \times 12 = 96$

× × × × × × × ×
× × × × × × × ×
× × × × × × × ×
× × × × × × × ×
× × × × × × × ×
× × × × × × × ×
× × × × × × × ×
× × × × × × × ×
× × × × × × × ×
× × × × × × × ×
× × × × × × × ×
× × × × × × × ×

Answer: 96 Books

Model Answers & Guidance

32. Shade ¾ of the following shape: (1)

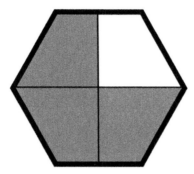

The student must shade in any three segments: it does not matter which one they leave blank.

33. The shape below has been divided into 4 equal sections.

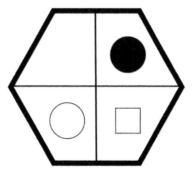

a) What fraction of the shape has a square in it? (1)

There is only one square present: contained within the bottom right quarter.

Answer: ¼

b) **What fraction of the shape has a black circle in it? (1)**

Answer: ¼

c) **What fraction does not have a shape in it? (1)**

Only one quarter — the top left quarter — does not contain a shape.

Answer: ¼

34. Sagar has 24 chocolates. He gives a quarter of them to his cousin.

How many chocolates does he have remaining for himself? (1)

18 chocolates

First, the student needs to realise that if Sagar gives away a quarter of his chocolates, he will have three quarters left.

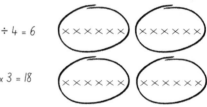

Next, to find a quarter, they need spilt 24 between 4 groups — and the number of chocolate in each group (6) is one quarter.

Finally, to find three quarters (the amount Sagar has left), we simply multiply 6 by 3 (=18).

Award one mark for the correct answer.

Answer: 18 Chocolates

35. Rajiv has £3.40 in his wallet and Ralph has 90p in his. How much money do they have in total? (1)

$$£3.40 + 90p = £4.30$$

£4.30

Your child may choose to solve this question using column addition – they must not forget to include the decimal point. If they chose to add the two numbers mentally, they could add £1 to £3.40 and then take away 10p.

Award one mark for the correct answer.

Answer: £4.30

36. Pierre buys a croissant that costs £3.30. He pays with a £5 note. How much change does he receive? (1)

$$£5.00 - £3.30 = £1.70$$

£1.70

The student could use the column subtraction method for this question. However, they may alternatively choose to answer the question mentally by counting the difference – 70p from £3.30 to £4 and then £1 to £5 (=£1.70).

Award one mark for the correct answer.

Answer: £1.70

37. Esther has £9.60 in her wallet. A bagel costs 90p. If she buys two bagels how much money will she have left? (2)

$$90p + 90p = £1.80$$

$$\begin{array}{r} £9.60 \\ - £1.80 \\ \hline £7.80 \end{array}$$

£7.80

This is a two-step word problem. First the student needs to find out how much money Esther is spending on bagels (=£1.80). Then they need to take away that total from the £9.60 she had in her wallet.

Award two marks for the correct answer and one mark if they got one part of the two calculations correct.

Model Answers & Guidance

Answer: £7.80

38. Round the following numbers to the nearest 10. (2)

a) 25   **30**

b) 79   **80**

Remember: if the number in the ones section is 1, 2, 3 or 4, you round down. If the number is 5, 6, 7, 8 or 9, you round up.

Award one mark for each correct answer.

39. Convert the following measurements: (2)

a) 2 ½ litres   **2500** millilitres

b) 3.5 metres   **350** centimetres.

Award one mark for each correct answer.

40. Underline the measurement that is closest in length to a bathtub: (1)

92m

12cm

1 ½ metres

300cm

This is a good opportunity to talk about centimetres and metres, and show your child with a tape measure what each measurement looks like.

Award one mark for the correct measurement being underlined.

41. Read the analogue clocks and write the time in digital form. (2)

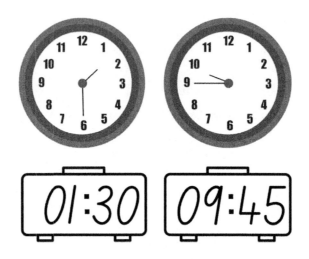

One mark for each correct answer.

Accept 13:30 for the left-hand clock. Accept 21:45 for the right-hand clock.

42. Convert the following periods of time: (2)

   a) 3 days   <u>72</u> hours

   b) ¾ of an hour   <u>45</u> minutes

Award one mark for each correct answer.

Model Answers & Guidance

43. Zach lives a 30 minute walk away from school. If he needs to be there by 8.30 am, what time does he need to leave his house? (1)

08:00 am

Discuss with the student whether they need to go back or forwards in time to find the answer. Get the student to think about where the minute hand will end up if they move back 30 minutes from 8.30 (it will then be on 12). Discuss where the hour hand would end up (=8).

Award one mark for the correct answer.

Answer: 08:00 am

44. Study the image below. Work out the rule and fill in the 3 missing numbers. (2)

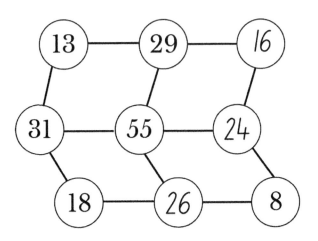

Whenever we have a chain of three numbers, connected by a sequence of lines, the central number is always the sum of the two on either side.

The key to working this out is the vertical chain on the left-hand side: 13 + 18 = 31.

From here, we can fill in the central number on the bottom row: we simply subtract 29 from 55, to give us 26. That 18 and 8 (the numbers in the bottom left and bottom right) add up to 26 confirms the pattern.

Award two marks for all answers being correct and one mark if at least 2 bubbles are correct.

45. Joshua has 6 different coins and each one is worth less than £1. What is the difference between the biggest and the smallest total she could have? (2)

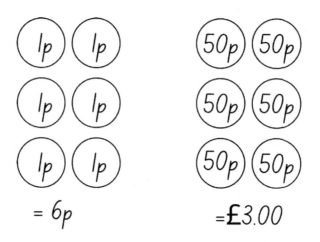

£3.00 - 6p = £2.94

£2.94

First establish which coins are the lowest and highest value coins under £1 (1p and 50p). Your child then needs to add up six 1p coins and six 20p coins. Finally, they need to find the difference between these two totals.

Award two marks for the correct answer and one mark if part of the answer is correct (e.g. finding the total of one set of four coins).

Answer: £2.94

46. Write the letter of the box that comes fifth in the sequence?
(1)

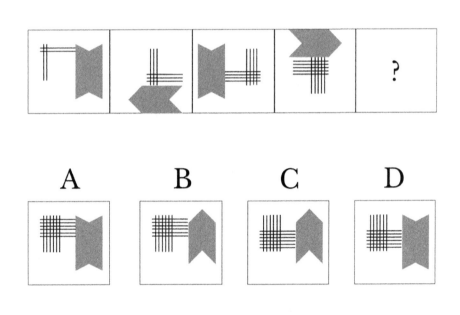

The first thing to note is that the solid shape moves clockwise with each step in the sequence: it goes from right, to bottom, to left, to top. As a result, we expect it to be on the right-hand side of the fifth figure.

However, whenever the solid shape is on the left- or right-hand side, it is not an arrow. Instead, both of its ends are indented. This means we can eliminate options B and C, as in both of these options, the solid shape is arrow-shaped.

The grid lines are rotating anti clockwise by 90 degrees with each new step — and two new lines are being added with each step. As a result, we expect them to be in the same state of rotation as the first title by the time we reach the fifth tile, but to contain 8 new lines. This describes option A, the correct answer.

Award one mark for identifying the correct tile.

Answer: A

47. Write the letter of the little box that finishes off the pattern in the big box. (1)

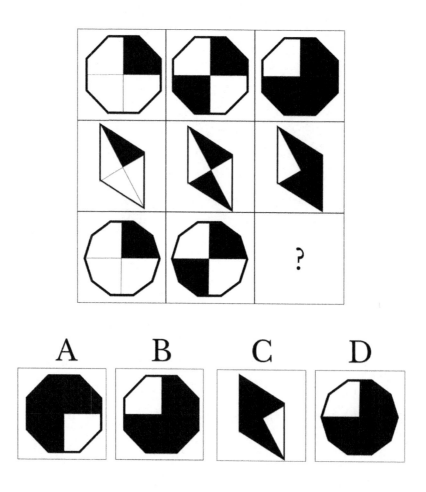

Each of the first two rows contains the same shape all three times. As a result, we would expect the third shape on the third row to be the same as the two to its left - which means we can eliminate options A, B and C, thereby leaving us with D.

But does option D work with the pattern of shading going on?

In the first column, the shape is always one quarter shaded. In the second column, it is always half shaded. And in the third column, it is always third shaded.

Since option D is also three quarters shaded, it does indeed fit with the pattern of shading here.

Award one mark for the correct shape being identified.

Answer: D

Paper Six: The Bit Of Everything Paper

As the name suggests, the Bit of Everything Paper is broad in scope and covers pretty much every topic your child will have covered at school (including shapes and angles).

This paper starts off with arithmetic questions that become incrementally more challenging. Your child should be able to answer the first few questions fairly quickly, thereby leaving them time to work on the paper's more complicated questions. Candidates are allotted 45 minutes to complete this paper, and there are 54 marks at stake.

The Bit Of Everything Paper
45 MINUTES: 21 QUESTIONS; 54 MARKS

1. Solve the following questions. (6)

15 - 3 = ____

5 + 4 = ____

15 – 7 = ____

7 + 7 + 9 = ____

7 x 3 = ____

12 x 5 = ____

2. Solve the questions below. Use the space provided to work out your answer. (4)

42 + 24 = ____

22 + 14 = ____

66 - 39 = ____

84 - 27 = ____

3. Fill in the missing numbers and symbols in the questions below. (4)

12 = 4 ____ 3

5 x ____ = 10

2 x 8 = 4 ____ 4

12 ____ 6 - 3 = 15

4. a. The rule for the number sequence below is add 6. Using this rule, continue the sequence. (1)

13, 19, 25, 31, 37, 43, ____ , ____

b. Find the rule for the number sequence below: (1)

29, 25, 21, 17, 13, 9, 5, 1

The rule is: _____

5. Order the numbers below from smallest to largest. (2)

| 4 | 92 | 23 | 177 | 203 | 123 | 34 |

| | | | | | | |

6. Look at the numbers below and find the following: (4)

| 26 | 96 | 78 | 74 | 84 | 35 | 21 | 13 | 39 |

The number that has 9 units____

The number that has 8 tens____

The numbers that are larger than 90 _____

The numbers that are less than 30_____

7. James baked 12 cookies, then gave 5 of them away. The next day, James baked 7 more cookies.

How many cookies does James end up with? (2)

Answer: _____

8. Tami is given four coins from her mum to spend on snacks. Together, they add up to 95p.

What are these four coins? (1)

Answer: _____

9. Hubert the maths tutor buys 26 special pencils and gives some of them to his students.

After this, Hubert has 5 pencils left.

How many pencils did he give away? (1)

Answer: _____

10. Ernie and Norma go to the pizza parlour.

Ernie buys a Margherita Pizza. Norma buys a Four Cheese Pizza. How much more does Norma spend? (1)

Answer: _____

11. Hennie bought 5 new books.

She paid with a £50 note and received £5 in change.

If all the books were the same price, how much did each book cost? (2)

Answer: _____

12. Underline all the shapes that are ¾ shaded. (2)

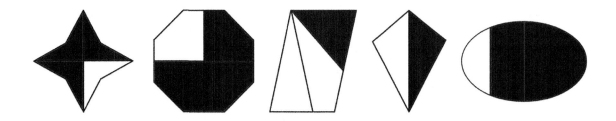

13. Shade in ¼ of the shape below. (1)

14. Label the shapes below: (3)

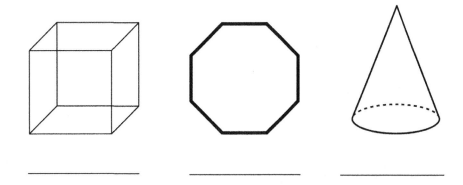

15. Match the items to approximately how much they weigh. (4)

A cat	200g
A mobile phone	12,000 kg
A horse	5 kg
A double decker bus	420 kg

16. Match the clock to the correct time. (4)

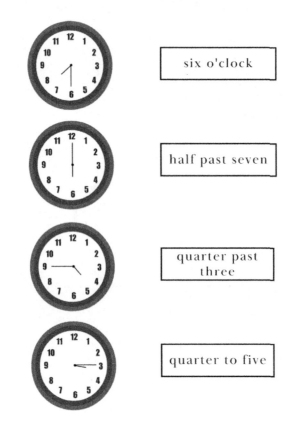

17. (1)

730 = 120 + 340 + ____

18. Circle the right angles in each of these shapes. (3)

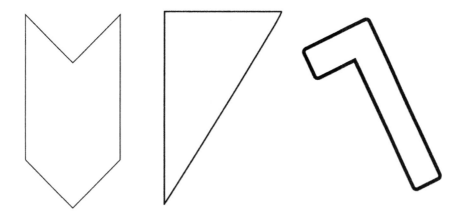

19. A group of students were asked which country in Europe they would most like to visit.

A chart showing the results can be found below.

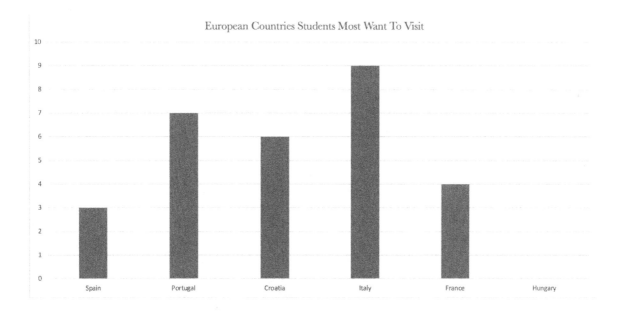

a) How many students chose Portugal? (1)

Answer: _____

b) Draw another bar on the chart to show that 7 students chose Hungary. (1)

20. A teacher decided to investigate how many pets her students owned. Complete the pictogram below and write the correct figure for the key. (4)

Type of Pet		Total
Dog	☐ ☐ ☐ ☐	16
Cat		28
Hamster	☐	
Goldfish		20

Key: ☐ = ____

21. Match the number the parrot calls out to the correct cracker. (1)

Model Answers & Guidance

1. Solve the following questions. (6)

15 - 3 = <u>12</u>

5 + 4 = <u>9</u>

15 − 7 = <u>8</u>

7 + 7 + 9 = <u>23</u>

7 x 3 = <u>21</u>

12 x 5 = <u>60</u>

Award one mark for each correct answer

2. Solve the questions below. Use the space provided to work out your answer. (4)

42 + 24 = <u>66</u>

Here the student should mentally add the tens and ones to find the answer.

---

22 + 14 = 36

Once again, mentally add the tens and ones.

---

66 - 39 = 27

If the candidate chooses to work out this question with mental arithmetic, I would suggest your child first takes away 9 from 66 (= 57) and then take away 3 tens (30) from 57. Alternatively, they could solve this question by writing it out using the column method.

---

84 - 27 = 57

Once again, take away the ones (7) from 84 (=77) and then take away the tens (20) from 77. Remember to encourage your child to check their answer by doing the inverse operation (does 57 + 27 equal 84?).

3. Fill in the missing numbers and symbols in the questions below. (4)

12 = 4 x 3

5 x 2 = 10

2 x 8 = 4 x 4

12 + 6 - 3 = 15

Model Answers & Guidance

Award one mark for each correct number/symbol.

4. a. The rule for the number sequence below is add 6. Using this rule, continue the sequence. (1)

13, 19, 25, 31, 37, 43, <u>49</u> , <u>55</u>

Award one mark for both numbers being correct.

b. Find the rule for the number sequence below: (1)

29, 25, 21, 17, 13, 9, 5, 1

The rule is: <u>*take away four*</u>

Accept any variation i.e. minus four, subtract four, four less, -4.

5. Order the numbers below from smallest to largest. (2)

| 4 | 92 | 23 | 177 | 203 | 123 | 34 |

| 4 | 23 | 34 | 92 | 123 | 177 | 203 |

Encourage your child to first look for all the single-digit numbers, then look at the two-digit numbers and finally look at the three-digit numbers.

Award two marks for all the numbers being in the correct positions and one mark if at least two of the digits are in the correct location.

6. Look at the numbers below and find the following: (4)

| 26 | 96 | 78 | 74 | 84 | 35 | 21 | 13 | 39 |

The number that has 9 units____

39

The number that has 8 tens____

84

The numbers that are larger than 90 _____

96

The numbers that are less than 30_____

26, 21, 13

7. James baked 12 cookies, then gave 5 of them away. The next day, James baked 7 more cookies.

How many cookies does James end up with? (2)

12 − 5 = 7

7 + 7 = 14

Model Answers & Guidance

14 cookies

This is a two-step word problem. The student first needs to work out how many cookies were left after James gave away 5 (=7); they then need to add to this number the number of cookies that James baked the next day (=7) to find the overall answer (=14).

Award two marks if your child had reached the answer of 14, and one mark if some of their working out was correct but the overall answer was incorrect.

Answer: 14 Cookies

8. Tami is given four coins from her mum to spend on snacks. Together, they add up to 95p.

What are these four coins? (1)

Award one mark for your child drawing the four coins above.

9. Hubert the maths tutor buys 26 special pencils and gives some of them to his students.

After this, Hubert has 5 pencils left.

How many pencils did he give away? (1)

---

26 - 5 = 21

This is a fairly straightforward subtraction question: we simply need to subtract 5 from 26 to derive our answer (=21).

Answer: 21 pencils

10. Ernie and Norma go to the pizza parlour.

Ernie buys a Margherita Pizza. Norma buys a Four Cheese Pizza. How much more does Norma spend? (1)

£13.70 - £7.90 = £5.80

£5.80

Here the student is being asked to find the difference between the amount of money Ernie and Norma spend. The key word here is 'more', which tell us we are comparing the two quantities.

Award one mark for the correct answer.

Answer: £5.80

11. Hennie bought 5 new books.

She paid with a £50 note and received £5 in change.

If all the books were the same price, how much did each book cost? (2)

£50 - £5 = £45

£45 ÷ 5 = £9

£9

This question is a bit more complex as we need to start at the end of the question. We first need to work out how much the four tickets cost altogether by working out how much Hennie paid for the books (=£45). We then need to divide that number by 5 to find out how much each book cost her (=£9).

Award full marks for the answer being correct and one mark if the answer is incorrect but some of the working out is correct.

Answer: £9

12. Underline all the shapes that are ¾ shaded. (2)

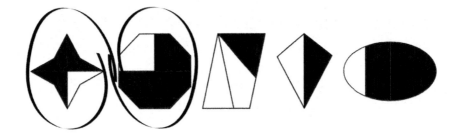

Sometimes the marks awarded for certain questions can give you a clue as to how many correct answers there are. This question awards two marks, since there are two shapes that are one third shaded.

13. Shade in ¼ of the shape below. (1)

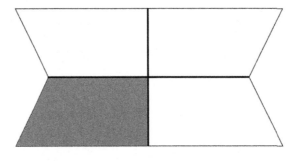

Award one mark for any variation where one of the four quarters are shaded.

14. Label the shapes below: (3)

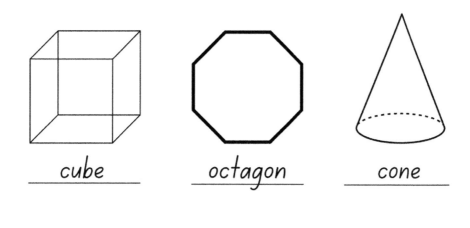

Award one mark for each correct shape name.

15. Match the items to approximately how much they weigh. (4)

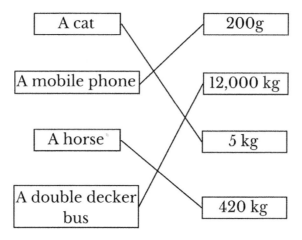

This is a good opportunity to explore how different units are used in different circumstances. Discuss how many grams there are in a kilogram, and why it would therefore be impractical to measure the weight of a double decker bus in grams, for example.

Award one mark for each correct answer.

16. Match the clock to the correct time. (4)

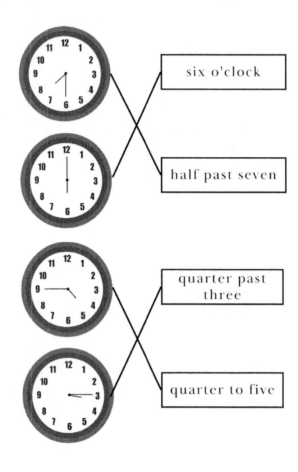

Award one mark for each correct answer.

17. (1)

   730 = 120 + 340 + <u>270</u>

Add 120 and 340 (=460) and then work out the difference between 730 and 460 (730 − 460 = 270).

18. Circle the right angles in each of these shapes. (3)

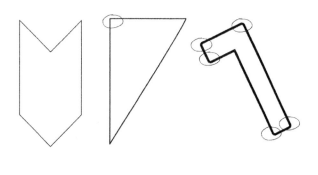

Recap the definition of a right angle – a 90° angle. Award three marks for all right angles being found, two marks if four out of the six are circled and one mark for three or less being circled.

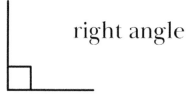

19. A group of students were asked which country in Europe they would most like to visit.

A chart showing the results can be found below.

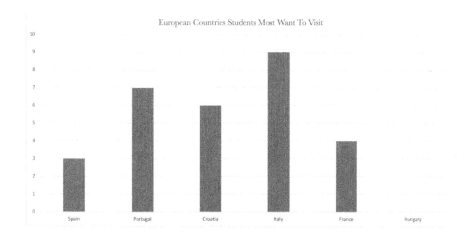

a) How many students chose Portugal? (1)

Answer: 7

b) Draw another bar on the chart to show that 7 students chose Hungary. (1)

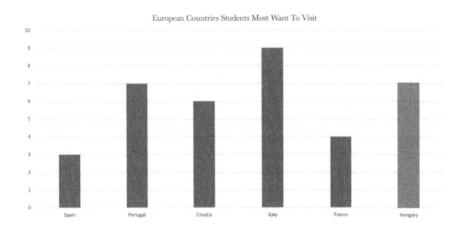

Award one mark for the correct marking on the bar chart (as shown above).

20. A teacher decided to investigate how many pets her students owned. Complete the pictogram below and write the correct figure for the key. (4)

Type of Pet		Total
Dog	☐☐☐☐	16
Cat	☐☐☐☐☐☐☐	28
Hamster	☐	4
Goldfish	☐☐☐☐☐	20

Key: ☐ = 4

Model Answers & Guidance

Look carefully at the information you are given. A sensible first step is to look at 'dog' as a choice – there are 4 squares, and a total number of 16 respondents, so we need to divide 16 by 4 to find out that each square represents 4 people. Using this information, we can then work out the missing parts to the pictogram.

When the total is present (as in with 28 cats), we need to complete the symbols to match this total; and when we are given the symbol, we need to count this up and write the total.

Award one mark for each part of the table being completed correctly; and one mark for writing that one square equals 4 in the key.

21. Match the number the parrot calls out to the correct cracker. (1)

Award one mark for the correct answer.

Paper Seven: The Multi-Parts, Multi-Steps Paper

The Multi-Step Paper stands out on the grounds that many of its questions are broken into multiple parts, thereby requiring students to go through multiple steps in order to complete the exercise.

To gain the full 64 marks, all the questions need to be answered correctly within the 40 minutes time frame, so you need to work fast. There is a lot to cover and this paper looks at a variety of topics, including bar charts, symmetry and coordinates.

The Multi-Parts, Multi-Steps Paper
40 MINS: 17 QUESTIONS, 64 MARKS

The question below has many parts to it. It is important that your child takes careful note of when they are being asked to calculate how many *individual* shoes as opposed to how many *pairs* of shoes.

1.

a) Samantha works in a shoe shop. Yesterday she sold 22 shoes. How many pairs was that? (1)

Answer: _____

b) Samantha's boss ordered 7 new pairs of trainers to sell in the store.

How many individual trainers did Samantha's boss order? (1)

Answer: _____

c) Today, Samantha was put in charge of the shoe display.

There were 14 shoes on display at the start of the day.

Samantha took down 7 old shoes and put up 9 new shoes.

How many shoes were on display once she was done. (1)

Answer: _____

d) Most of the shoes are stored on shelves at the back of the store.

Each shelf can hold 6 shoes.

How many shelves are needed to hold 30 shoes? (1)

Answer: _____

e) How many shelves will be needed for 45 shoes? (1)

Answer: _____

f) Samantha's boss builds 6 larger shelves at the front of the store.

Each of these larger shelves can hold 8 shoes.

How many shoes in total can be stored at the front of the store? (1)

Answer: _____

2.

a) Danielle is given 3 gold stars for every 2 hours she spends studying.

On Monday, Danielle spent 6 hours studying.

How many gold stars did Danielle receive on Monday? (1)

Answer: _____

b) Last week, Danielle was given 27 gold stars.

How many hours did she spend studying last week? (1)

Answer: _____

3.

a) Terry and Jane both love the long jump. Terry can jump 154cm and Jane can jump 177cm. How much further can Jane jump than Terry? (1)

Answer: _____

b) There are 32 children on the athletics team.

Unfortunately, a quarter of the children are not free to attend the upcoming tournament.

How many members of the team are free to attend the tournament? (1)

Answer: _____

c) Before the tournament, Terry and Jane plan to train 3 times a day for 3 weeks.

How many training sessions will they have? (1)

Answer: _____

4. Solve the following questions: (11)

a) 9 + 4 = ____

b) 12 - 7 = ____

c) 16 + 7 = ____

d) 17 - 6 = ____

e) 54 + 8 = ____

f) 78 - 12 = ____

g) 9 x 9 = ____

h) 30 x 4 = ____

i) 15 + 7 + 6 = ____

j) 13 + 7 - 5 = ____

k) 37 - 3 + 13 = ____

5. Fill in the missing sign: + - x ÷ (3)

$8 \;\square\; 4 = 2$ $\qquad$ $14 \;\square\; 14 = 1$

$7 \;\square\; 0 = 0$ $\qquad$ $5 \;\square\; 5 = 25$

$13 \;\square\; 13 = 26$ $\qquad$ $49 \;\square\; 25 = 24$

6. Fill in the missing numbers below. (4)

```
   5 □              7 3
 + □ 5            - 2 □
 ──────          ──────
   1 0 8            4 7


     4 7              2 7
 x   □ 5          x   □
 ──────          ──────
   2 □ 5            1 □ 9
```

7. Fill in the missing numbers in the sequences (3)

78, 71, ___, 57, ___, 43, 36, ___

1, 3, 9, ___, ___, 243

0, 2, 6, 12, 20, ___, 42, ___, 72

8. Claire decided to find out how many books each of her friends had read over the past year. She jots her findings in the bar chart below:

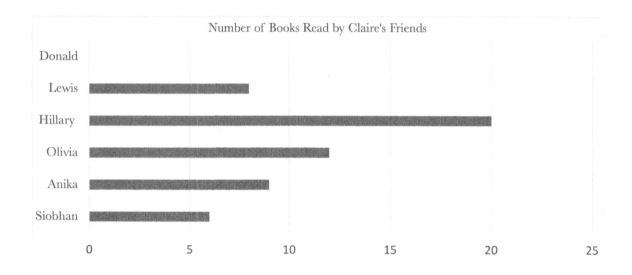

a. How many books did Hillary read? (1)

Answer: _____

b. Estimate how many books Olivia read. (1)

Answer: _____

9. Lizzie went to the pet shop with her pocket money. She had one £1 coin and one 50p coin to spend on her cat.

The following items were available.

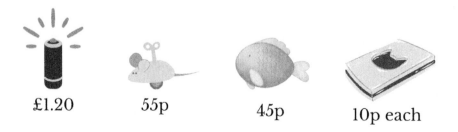

£1.20   55p   45p   10p each

a. If Lizzie wants to buy one of each item, is she able to? (1)

Answer: _____

b. What would the laser point, the fish toy and a single cat biscuit cost? (1)

Answer: _____

c. Lizzie decides to spend just £1. If she buys the fish toy, how many cat biscuits can she buy? (2)

Answer: _____

d. In the end, Lizzie decides that she will use her £1 to buy a fish toy and a single cat biscuit. How much will she spend in total? (1)

Answer: _____

e. Lizzie hands over her £1 and is given 3 coins change. What are these three coins? (1)

Answer: _____

f. Imagine instead that Lizzie spent £1.20 on FOUR things.

Which four things would she have bought? (2)

Answer: _____

10. This is Robert the Robot.

Draw his twin brother, Flexo, using the line of symmetry down the middle. (3)

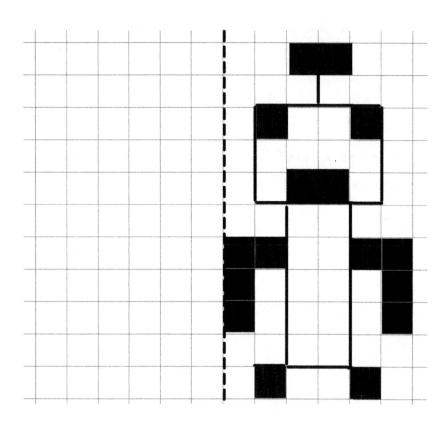

11.

a) Tony's watch is running 15 minutes fast.

It currently reads 7:00.

Draw hands on the analogue clock to show the correct time. (1)

b) Paul leaves home at 8:45.

School starts 45 minutes later.

Draw hands on the analogue clock to show when Paul's school starts. (1)

c) Jason is running 15 minutes late for his 1.15 lunch booking.

Draw hands on the analogue clock to show when Jason will arrive. (1)

12. What time do you eat breakfast?

Draw hands on the analogue clock. (1)

13. Read the times on the clock faces and write them in digital form. (2)

14. Claude loves to draw shapes. Complete the tasks below. (3)

a. He wants you to draw a shape on the grid below with the following coordinates. Plot each one and join it to the next: (1,6), (5,9), (9,6), (8,1), (2,1), (1,6).

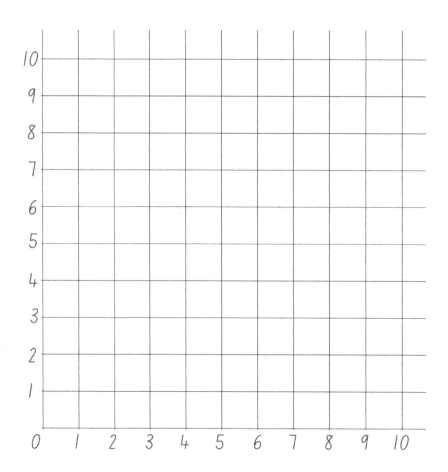

b) What is the name of the shape Claude has asked you to draw?

Answer: _____

c) Claude now wants you to draw a square within the shape you have just drawn, choosing 4 points on the grid.

Write the coordinates of the points you chose.

(__ , __), (__ , __), (__ , __), (__ , __)

15. Count the squares and triangles in the picture below. (2)

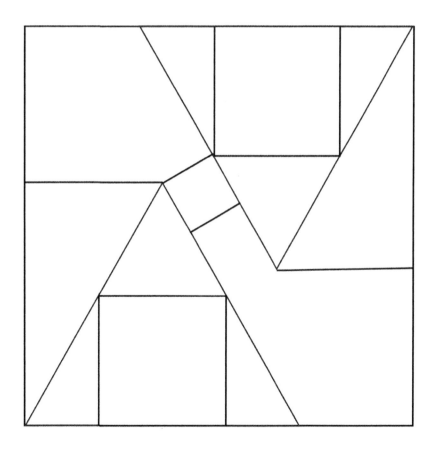

Squares: _____ ; Triangles _____

16. Errol the Explorer visits the nation of Podmania.

In Podmania, the money used is Pods and Octopods.

8 Pods are worth 1 Octopod.

    a) Why do you think it is called an Octopod? (1)

    Answer: _____

_____

    b) How many Pods is 2 Octopods + 5 Pods? (1)

                                                       Answer: _____

    c) Change 37 Pods into Octopods and Pods. (1)

                                                       Answer: _____

    d) Errol has 6 Octopods.

    What change will he be given if he spends 3 Octopods and 2 Pods. (1)

                                                       Answer: _____

17. Look at each of the pictures below and write a fraction to represent the shaded part of each picture. (4)

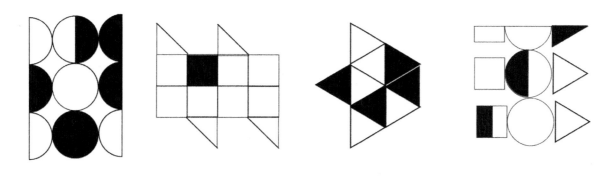

_____   _____   _____   _____

Model Answers & Guidance

The question below has many parts to it. It is important that your child takes careful note of when they are being asked to calculate how many *individual* shoes as opposed to how many *pairs* of shoes.

1.

a) Samantha works in a shoe shop. Yesterday she sold 22 shoes. How many pairs was that? (1)

22 ÷ 2 = 11

<u>11</u> pairs of shoes

Your child may choose to use a drawing to help them visualise this question. At any rate, as long as they land on the correct answer, award one mark.

Answer: 11 pairs of shoes

b) Samantha's boss ordered 7 new pairs of trainers to sell in the store.

How many individual trainers did Samantha's boss order? (1)

7 x 2 = 14

14 shoes

Answer: 14 shoes

c) Today, Samantha was put in charge of the shoe display.

There were 14 shoes on display at the start of the day.

Samantha took down 7 old shoes and put up 9 new shoes.

How many shoes were on display once she was done. (1)

14 − 7 = 7

7 + 9 = 16

16 shoes

Award one mark for the correct answer.

Answer: 16 shoes

d) Most of the shoes are stored on shelves at the back of the store.

Each shelf can hold 6 shoes.

How many shelves are needed to hold 30 shoes? (1)

$30 \div 6 = 5$

5 shelves

One mark for the correct answer.

Answer: 5 shelves

e) How many shelves will be needed for 45 shoes? (1)

8 shelves

This question is looking to see that your child can apply their times tables knowledge to find the best fit answer – they know that 6 goes into 45 seven times but then they will have some shoes left over, so the shop would need to use one extra shelf (=8 shelves).

Award one mark for the correct answer.

Answer: 8 shelves

f) Samantha's boss builds 6 larger shelves at the front of the store.

Each of these larger shelves can hold 8 shoes.

How many shoes in total can be stored at the front of the store? (1)

$6 \times 8 = 48$

48 shoes

Award one mark for the correct answer.

Answer: 48 shoes

2.

a) Danielle is given 3 gold stars for every 2 hours she spends studying.

On Monday, Danielle spent 6 hours studying.

How many gold stars did Danielle receive on Monday? (1)

$6 \div 2 = 3$

$3 \times 3 = 9$

9 gold stars

---

3 gold stars every 2 hours. Since there are 3 lots of two hours in six hours, we need to multiply 3 by 3 — this amounts to the total number of gold stars Danielle receives on Monday.

Award one mark for the correct answer.

Answer: <u>9 gold stars</u>

b) Last week, Danielle was given 27 gold stars.

How many hours did she spend studying last week? (1)

27 ÷ 3 = 9

9 x 2 = 18

<u>18</u> hours

We know that Danielle gets 3 gold stars for every two hours, so if we divide the 27 gold stars by 3, we find out how many two hour long sessions Danielle put in (=9).

To find out how many hours this is in total, we simply multiply 9 by 2 (=18).

Award one mark for the correct answer.

Answer: <u>18 hours</u>

3.

a) Terry and Jane both love the long jump.

Terry can jump 154cm and Jane can jump 177cm.

How much further can Jane jump than Terry? (1)

<u>23</u> cm

The key is to understand that this question is asking your child to compare the two distances and find the difference.

Award one mark for the correct answer.

```
  1 7 7
- 1 5 4
-------
  0 2 3
```

Answer: 23 cm

b) There are 32 children on the athletics team.

Unfortunately, a quarter of the children are not free to attend the upcoming tournament.

How many members of the team <u>are</u> free to attend the tournament? (1)

32 ÷ 4 = 8

8 x 3 = 24

<u>24 children</u>

Your child may decide to mentally halve 32 and halve it again to find a quarter (=8). Then they simply need to multiply this figure by 3 in order to find three quarters. Award one mark for the correct answer.

Answer: <u>24 children</u>

c) Before the tournament, Terry and Jane plan to train 3 times a day for 3 weeks.

How many training sessions will they have? (1)

7 x 3 = 21

3 x 21 = 63

63 times

Award one mark for the correct answer.

Answer: 63 times

4. Solve the following questions: (11)

a) 9 + 4 = 13

b) 12 - 7 = 5

c) 16 + 7 = 23

d) 17 - 6 = 11

e) 54 + 8 = 62

f) 78 - 12 = 66

g) 9 x 9 = __81__

h) 30 x 4 = __120__

i) 15 + 7 + 6 = __28__

j) 13 + 7 - 5 = __15__

k) 37 - 3 + 13 = __47__

One mark for each correct answer. Discuss how they could calculate any questions they answered incorrectly.

5. Fill in the missing sign: + - x ÷ (3)

$$8 \; \boxed{\times} \; 4 = 2 \qquad 14 \; \boxed{\div} \; 14 = 1$$

$$7 \; \boxed{\div \text{ or } \times} \; 0 = 0 \qquad 5 \; \boxed{\times} \; 5 = 25$$

$$13 \; \boxed{+} \; 13 = 26 \qquad 49 \; \boxed{-} \; 25 = 24$$

Make sure to discuss the reasons behind the questions 7 x/÷ 0 = 0 (in other words, why we could use either a division or multiplication sign).

Award three marks if all the answers are correct. Award two marks if at least half the answers are correct and one mark if only one or two answers are correct.

6. Fill in the missing numbers below. (4)

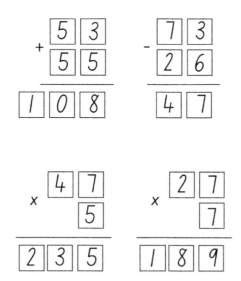

TOP LEFT: this question is straightforward – your child simply needs to work out what they need to add to 5 to make 8 (=3) and then what they need to add to 5(0) to make 10(0) (=5(0)).

TOP RIGHT: there is no number you can take away from 3 to make 7, therefore it is clear that you need to borrow a ten from 'next door'. That then means that the number under the 3 needs to be 6. Encourage your child to double check their answers when they are done!

BOTTOM LEFT: multiply 7 and 5 (=35). Put the three under the tens section and then work out the rest to see what needs to go in the missing section.

BOTTOM RIGHT: start by working out what number you need to multiply by 7 to make a number that ends in 9 (=7). Then continue to work out the answer to the next missing section.

Award one mark for each correct answer.

7. Fill in the missing numbers in the sequences (3)

78, 71, _64_, 57, _50_, 43, 36, _29_ (−7)

1, 3, 9, _27_, _81_, 243 (×3)

0, 2, 6, 12, 20, _30_, 42, _56_, 72 (+2, +4, +6, +8, +10, +12, +14, +16)

As always, before filling in the missing numbers in the sequences, you need to work out the 'jump' sizes or pattern. For the first sequence, the numbers are going down in 7s. In the second sequence, the numbers are increasing in multiples of 3. In the final sequence, the jump between each number is increasing by 2 each time. Award one mark for each correct sequence.

8. Claire decided to find out how many books each of her friends had read over the past year. She jots her findings in the bar chart below:

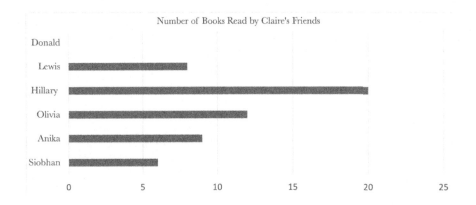

a) How many books did Hillary read? (1)

Model Answers & Guidance

20 books

The bar representing the books Hillary read is clearly on 20. Award a mark for the correct answer.

Answer: 20 books

b) **Estimate how many books Olivia read. (1)**

The bar for Olivia is just shy of the halfway mark between 10 and 15 which means it is 12; however, if the student has written 13, they should still be awarded the mark as they have managed to make an estimate that is close enough to the correct answer.

Answer: 12 books

9. Lizzie went to the pet shop with her pocket money. She had one £1 coin and one 50p coin to spend on her cat.

The following items were available.

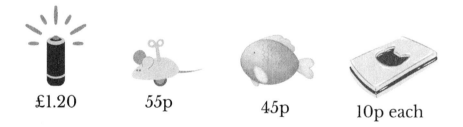

£1.20   55p   45p   10p each

a) **If Lizzie wants to buy one of each item, is she able to? (1)**

yes / no

It would not be possible as she has £1.50 to spend and just buying a laser pointer and the fish toy, for instance, already takes her to £1.65.

Award one mark for circling/underlining 'no'.

b) What would the laser point, the fish toy and a single cat biscuit cost? (1)

10p + 45p + 120p = 175p OR £1.75

£1.75

Award one mark for the correct answer.

Answer: £1.75

c) Lizzie decides to spend just £1. If she buys the fish toy, how many cat biscuits can she buy? (2)

100p − 45p = 55p

55p ÷ 10p = 5 (remainder 5)

5 biscuits

You first take away the cost of the fish toy (45p) from the 100p/£1 she has to spend, which gives you 55p. You then see how many 10p biscuits Lizzie can buy for 55p.

Award two marks for correctly answering '5' and one mark if some of the working out is correct but the final answer is wrong.

Model Answers & Guidance

Answer: 5 biscuits

d) In the end, Lizzie decides that she will use her £1 to buy a fish toy and a single cat biscuit. How much will she spend in total? (1)

45p + 10p = 55p

55p

Answer: 55p

e) Lizzie hands over her £1 and is given 3 coins change.

What are these three coins? (1)

Remember, this is the change given from the £1 (or 100p) she has decided to spend out of her £1.50 pocket money.

Award one mark for any variation of coins that equates to 45p.

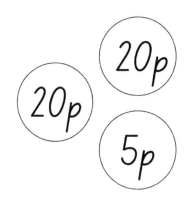

f) Imagine instead that Lizzie spent £1.20 on FOUR things.

Which four things would she have bought? (2)

One cat toy, one fish toy, and two biscuits.

We start off with what we know and common sense:

1. We know Lizzie cannot afford to buy the laser pointer as she has £1.20 to spend on four items and the laser pointer alone is £1.20.

2. She is buying four items so this must be a mixture of items as four lots of one item will either be more than £1.20 or less than £1.20.

Next take the highest priced item (after the laser pointer), which is the mouse toy, and add the next highest priced item (the fish toy) — this equals £1.00 (at this point two items have been 'bought'). Then check whether adding two biscuits (taking us to four items) gets us to £1.20 – which it does.

Award two marks if all correct items are listed and one mark if most are.

Answer: one cat toy, one fish toy, and two biscuits.

10. This is Robert the Robot.

Draw his twin brother, Flexo, using the line of symmetry down the middle. (3)

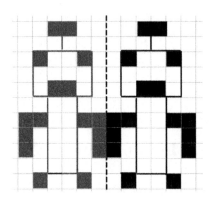

Tip: get your child to look at one row at a time. Carefully count how many boxes away from the centre line each square or line is to the right and then draw a line/square at the same distance but to the left.

Model Answers & Guidance

Award 3 marks for all the lines and squares being in the correct place, 2 marks if most are and 1 mark if only a few are correct.

11.

a) Tony's watch is running 15 minutes fast.

It currently reads 7:00.

Draw hands on the analogue clock to show the correct time. (1)

First establish whether you need to add or take away time from 7:00. The answer here is 6:45 so your child must ensure the hour hand is between 6 and 7 (though closer to 7), and the minute hand points to 9.

Award one mark for drawing the hands in the correct positions.

b) Paul leaves home at 8:45.

School starts 45 minutes later.

Draw hands on the analogue clock to show when Paul's school starts. (1)

Once again, establish if you need to add or take away time before drawing the hands in the correct positions for 9:30pm.

c) Jason is running 15 minutes late for his 1.15 lunch booking.

Draw hands on the analogue clock to show when Jason will arrive. (1)

Fifteen minutes is a quarter turn around the clock face (for the minutes hand), so begin by thinking about where the hands would be for 1:15pm (minute hand on 3) and then move the minute hand a quarter way round (so it points to 6). Meanwhile, make sure the hour hand moves to a position roughly between 1 and 2.

Award one mark for the hands correctly positioned to show the time 1:30.

12. What time do you eat breakfast?

Draw hands on the analogue clock. (1)

Accept any time between 7am and 11am – if they are trying to show half past the hour, make sure the hour hand is in between two hours (for instance, for half past 7, the hour hand should be between 7 and 8).

. . .

Model Answers & Guidance 205

13. Read the times on the clock faces and write them in digital form. (2)

Award one mark for each correct answer. Accept 24 hour times – 14:50 and 20:25.

14. Claude loves to draw shapes. Complete the tasks below. (3)

a. He wants you to draw a shape on the grid below with the following coordinates. Plot each one and join it to the next: (1,6), (5,9), (9,6), (8,1), (2,1), (1,6)

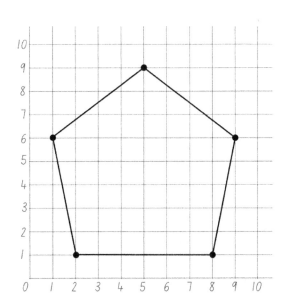

b) What is the name of the shape Claude has asked you to draw?

We have a five-sided shape, and this is known as a pentagon.

Answer: Pentagon

c) Claude now wants you to draw a square within the shape you have just drawn, choosing 4 points on the grid.

Write the coordinates of the points you chose.

$(4, 2), (4, 4), (6, 4), (6, 2)$

There is no single correct answer here. Rather, any four coordinates that combine to create a square within the pentagon will be accepted.

The square I have chosen is 2 squares by 2 squares. However, a smaller square (for instance, one that is the size of a single grid box) or a large one (for instance, one that is 4 squares by 4 squares in dimensions) would also be credited.

15. Count the squares and triangles in the picture below. (2)

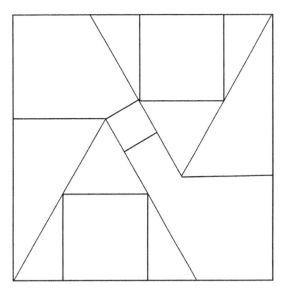

Squares: 4; Triangles: 8

When counting the squares, make sure to remember to count the large one that encompasses all the other shapes.

Award two marks for correctly identifying the total for each shape, and one mark if only one total is correct.

Answer: <u>Squares: 4; Triangles: 8</u>

16. Errol the Explorer visits the nation of Podmania.

In Podmania, the money used is Pods and Octopods.

8 Pods are worth 1 Octopod.

    a) Why do you think it is called an Octopod? (1)

I think it is called an Octopod because putting 'octo' at the front of a word indicates that it is to do with the number eight.

OR

A shape with eight sides is called an Octagon, so it makes sense that an Octopod would contain eight units.

OR

An octopus is an animal with eight legs. Octopod also starts with 'octo', so it makes sense that it contains eight units

---

The examiner is looking to see whether students understand that 'octo-' means eight. They can either say this explicitly, like in my first example answer. Or they can demonstrate it implicitly, by bringing up another word that contains 'octo' and refers to the number eight.

b) How many Pods is 2 Octopods + 5 Pods? (1)

We know that 1 Octopod equates to 8 Pods.

As a result, 2 Octopods equates to 8 x 2 Pods (=16 Pods).

We then need to add the 5 extra Pods to these 16 Pods.

16 + 5 = 21 Pods

Answer: 21 Pods

c) Change 37 Pods into Octopods and Pods. (1)

$37 \div 8 = 4$, remainder 5.

4 Octopods and 5 Pods.

Since there are 8 Pods to an Octopod, we need to divide 37 Pods by 8 to discover how many Octopods we have (=4).

However, we then have 5 Pods left over. Therefore, we have 4 Octopods and 5 Pods.

Answer: <u>4 Octopods and 5 Pods.</u>

d) Errol has 6 Octopods.

What change will he be given if he spends 3 Octopods and 2 Pods. (1)

$6 - 3^2/_8 = 2^6/_8$

Our first step is to subtract 3 Octopods from the total of 6 Octopods. This leaves us with 3 Octopods.

We then need to subtract 2 Pods from 3 Octopods

As there are 8 Pods in an Octopods, this leaves us with 2 Octopods and 6 Pods in change.

The student will also be credited if they state that Errol will receive 22 Pods in change (which is the equivalent of 2 Octopods and 6 Pods).

Answer: <u>2 Octopods and 6 Pods</u>

17. Look at each of the pictures below and write a fraction to represent the shaded part of each picture. (4)

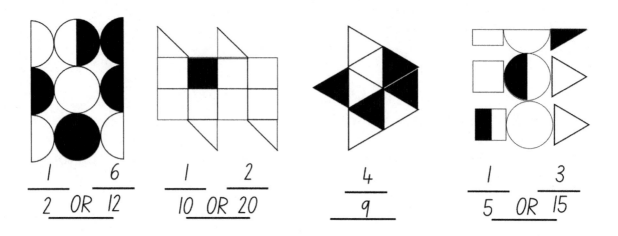

Picture 1: Ask your child to look at the shape as being made up entirely of semi-circles (12 semi-circles). In all, 6 semi-circles are shaded. As a result, $6/12$, or $1/2$ is shaded.

Picture 2: Ask your child to think of the shape as being made up entirely of triangles formed from diagonally cut squares (20 triangles). In all, 2 triangles are shaded. As a result, $2/20$, or $1/10$ is shaded.

Picture 3: There are 9 identically sized triangles in total, 4 of which are shaded. This equates to $4/9$ shaded.

Picture 4: Here we have a shape that is made up of 5 half squares, 5 semi-circles, and 5 triangles (we are mentally splitting the unshaded triangles into two). $1/5$ of the semi-circles are shaded. $1/5$ of the half squares have been shaded. $1/5$ of the half triangles have been shaded. As a result, the total area shaded is $1/5$.

Award one mark for each correct answer.

Paper Eight: The Thematic Paper

The Thematic Paper is laid out a little differently to the others. It explores areas more thematically. So, for example, addition/subtraction arithmetic problems are followed by addition/subtraction word problems. Then this pattern is repeated for multiplication/division problems — you have arithmetic problems, then word problems — and so on in this vein!

This is an extensive paper and there is a lot to cover in 45 minutes. It is important your child works quickly, but also takes care not to lose marks by making mistakes that could have been avoided.

The Thematic Paper
45 MINS: 27 QUESTIONS, 84 MARKS

1. Write the numbers below in digit form: (4)

seventeen _____

fifty two _____

four hundred and thirty three   _____

seven hundred and seven   _____

2. Order the numbers below from smallest to largest: (2)

88   4   52   91   39   87

_____

13   41   3   70   77   55

_____

3. Continue the number sequences below: (3)

40, 35, 30, 25, ___ , ___

24, 22, 20, 18, ___ , ___

591, 592, 593, ___ , ___

4. a. Write three numbers between 15 and 30 that are even. (3)

_____

b. Write three numbers between 35 and 50 that are odd. (3)

_____

5. Solve the following additions: (8)

a) 92 + 1 = ___

b) 89 + 1 = ___

c) 229 + 1 = ___

d) 65 + 10 = ___

e) 445 + 10 = ___

f) 503 + 10 = ___

g) 337 + 100 = ___

h) 625 + 100 = ___

6. Fill in the missing numbers: (3)

$$16 + \boxed{} = 23$$

$$\boxed{} + 7 = 14$$

$$4 + \boxed{} + 6 = 18$$

7. Solve the following subtractions: (6)

a) 19 - 4 = _____

b) 15 - 6 = _____

c) 9 less than 31 = _____

d) 57 - 6 = _____

e) 74 - 28 = _____

f) **Find the difference between 35 and 7.** _____

8. Fill in the missing numbers: (5)

$7 - 5 = \square$

$\square - 5 = 9$

$8 - \square = 3$

$8 - 6 + 7 = \square$

$3 + 8 - 2 = \square$

9. Calculate the answers to the following: (6)

```
   7 7        6 3       1 2 9
+  1 2     +  2 7    +    6 8
 -----      -----      ------
```

```
   8 7        6 6        7 4
-    4     -  2 4     -  4 9
 -----      -----      ------
```

10. Trevor eats 9 grapes before lunch and 4 grapes after lunch.

    a) How many grapes has Trevor eaten in total? (1)

Answer: _____

    b) How many more grapes did Trevor eat before lunch compared to after lunch? (1)

Answer: _____

11. Loraine has 11 chocolate buttons.

    a) If Loraine gives 5 chocolates to her sister, how many does she have left? (1)

Answer: _____

    b) If Loraine then eats 4 chocolates, how many does she have left? (1)

Answer: _____

12. Henry has 5 fewer marbles than Fiona, who has 11 marbles. How many marbles does Henry have? (1)

Answer: _____

13. Solve the following: (9)

a) 8 x 2 = _____

b) 3 x 5 = _____

c) 6 lots of 6 = _____

d) 4 multiplied by 7 = _____

e) How many are nine fours? = _____

f) How many 4s are there in 20? _____

g) Divide 9 by 3 = _____

h) Share 20 lollipops among 4 children = _____

i) 65 ÷ 5 = _____

14. There are 5 children on each basketball team

There are 5 teams in the league.

How many children are there in the league in total? (1)

Answer: _____

15. Toby needs to put his yo-yo collection into storage. He has 42 yo-yos. An empty shoe box can hold 6 yo-yos.

How many shoe boxes does Toby need to package up his entire collection? (1)

Answer: _____

16. Daria has 9 conkers. Quinn has twice as many. How many conkers does Quinn have? (1)

Answer: _____

17. Look at shapes A-F. (3)

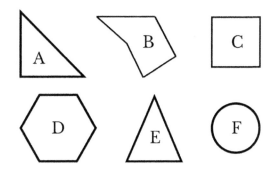

a) **Which is the pentagon?**

Answer: _____

b) **Which is the hexagon?**

Answer: _____

c) **Which is the right-angled triangle?**

Answer: _____

18. Shade half of this triangle: (1)

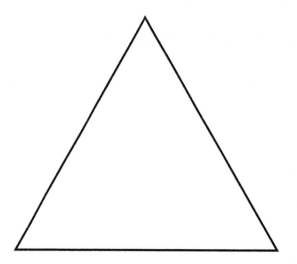

19.

  a) Name 3 coins that add up to 22p (1)

  _____

  b) Name 3 coins that add up to 41p (1)

  _____

20. Lawrence had two 50 pence coins. He spent 73p on a can of cola. How much change did he receive? (1)

Answer: _____

21. How much is:

a) Seven 5p coins and three 20p coins? (1)

Answer: _____

b) Eight 2p coins and seven 10p coins? (1)

Answer: _____

22. Lucy and Leiliah decided to count their pocket money. (4)

a. Write the total underneath each piggy bank.

_____   _____

b. Who has more money? _____

c. How much more? _____

d. How much do the children have in total? _____

23. Ada asked her classmates whether they prefer baths or showers, and kept a tally.

shower	baths
𝍷𝍷𝍷 𝍷𝍷𝍷 𝍷𝍷𝍷 𝍷𝍷𝍷 𝍷𝍷𝍷 𝍷	𝍷𝍷𝍷 𝍷𝍷𝍷 𝍷𝍷

How many more people preferred a shower compared to those who preferred a bath? (1)

_____ **points**

24. Lance runs a YouTube channel.

The graph below shows how many views his most recent video received per day over the past week.

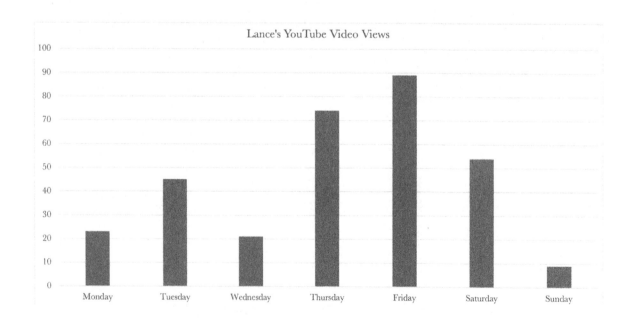

a) On which day did Lance's video receive the most views? (1)

Answer: _____

b) On which day did Lance's video receive the least views? (1)

Answer: _____

25. **Caroline runs a sauce shop.**

Here is a graph representing the number of sales she made yesterday

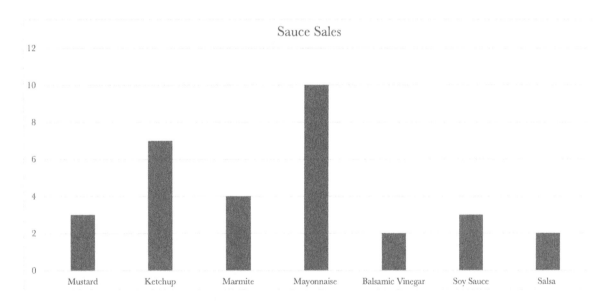

a) How many units of marmite did she sell? (1)

Answer: _____

b) How many units of ketchup did she sell? (1)

Answer: _____

26. Look at the image below. (3)

a) How many 'L' shapes are there?

Answer: _____

b) How many 'C' shapes are there?

Answer: _____

c) Are there more circles or more lines?

Answer: _____

27. Write the numbers shown on these abaci. (3)

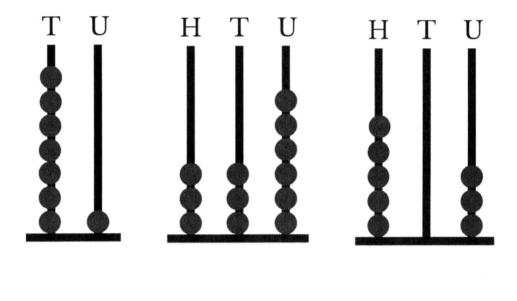

_____   _____   _____

Model Answers & Guidance

1. Write the numbers below in digit form: (4)

seventeen

17

fifty two

52

four hundred and thirty three

433

seven hundred and seven

707

Award one mark for each correct answer.

2. Order the numbers below from smallest to largest: (2)

88   4   52   91   39   87

4   39   52   87   88   91

13   41   3   70   77   55

3   13   41   55   70   77

This question looks to see whether your child understands the importance of place value. Firstly they must place the numbers that are single-digit, then they need to look at the two-digit numbers, focusing on the tens and then the ones.

Award one mark for each group of numbers that is ordered correctly.

3. Continue the number sequences below: (3)

40, 35, 30, 25, *20*, *15*

24, 22, 20, 18, *16*, *14*

591, 592, 593, *594*, *595*

Look carefully at each sequence, establish the rule – are the numbers going up or down and by how much?

Award one mark for each sequence that has been completed correctly.

4. a. Write three numbers between 15 and 30 that are even. (3)

Recap what we mean by even – any number that can be divided into two equal groups (numbers ending in 0, 2, 4, 6 and 8).

Award a mark for each one of the following numbers the candidate offers: 16, 18, 20, 22, 24, 26, 28.

b. Write three numbers between 35 and 50 that are odd. (3)

Recap what we mean by odd – any number that cannot be divided into two equal groups (numbers ending in 1, 3, 5, 7 and 9).

Award one mark for each of the following answers 37, 39, 41, 43, 45, 47, 49.

5. Solve the following additions: (8)

a) 92 + 1 = **93**

b) 89 + 1 = **90**

c) 229 + 1 = **230**

d) 65 + 10 = **75**

e) 445 + 10 = **455**

f) 503 + 10 = <u>513</u>

g) 337 + 100 = <u>437</u>

h) 625 + 100 = <u>725</u>

These questions require the student to use mental addition strategies.

Award one mark for each correct answer.

6. Fill in the missing numbers: (3)

$$16 + \boxed{7} = 23$$

$$\boxed{7} + 7 = 14$$

$$4 + \boxed{8} + 6 = 18$$

All the calculations above require the use of inverse calculations to find the answer – take away the addends (numbers to the left of the equals sign) from the sum (number to the right of the equals sign) to find the missing number.

Award one mark for each correct answer.

Model Answers & Guidance

7. Solve the following subtractions: (6)

    a) 19 - 4 = <u>15</u>

    b) 15 - 6 = <u>9</u>

    c) 9 less than 31 = <u>22</u>

    d) 57 - 6 = <u>51</u>

    e) 74 - 28 = <u>46</u>

    f) Find the difference between 35 and 7 = <u>28</u>

The questions above require your child to use mental strategies to subtract. Award one mark for each correct answer.

8. Fill in the missing numbers: (5)

$$7 - 5 = \boxed{2}$$
$$\boxed{14} - 5 = 9$$
$$8 - \boxed{5} = 3$$
$$8 - 6 + 7 = \boxed{9}$$
$$3 + 8 - 2 = \boxed{9}$$

Award one mark for each correct answer.

9. Calculate the answers to the following: (6)

```
  77         63        129
+ 12       + 27       + 68
  ──         ──        ───
  89         90        197
```

```
  87         66        ⁶7̶4
-  4       - 24       - 49
  ──         ──        ──
  83         42        25
```

The questions above get increasingly harder for each operation (as you go from left to right). The examiner is looking to see whether the student can tackle different types of column method addition and subtraction questions – including ones where they have to carry over and borrow.

Award one mark for each calculation that is solved correctly.

10. Trevor eats 9 grapes before lunch and 4 grapes after lunch.

a) How many grapes has Trevor eaten in total? (1)

<u>13</u> grapes

Model Answers & Guidance

The student may choose to write out the calculation 9 + 4 = 13, or they might solve this part of the problem mentally.

Answer: 13 grapes

b) How many more grapes did Trevor eat before lunch compared to after lunch? (1)

5 grapes

Once again, this part of the question can be easily solved mentally so there is no need to write down the calculation.

Answer: 5 grapes

11. Loraine has 11 chocolate buttons.

a) If Loraine gives 5 chocolates to her sister, how many does she have left? (1)

Answer: 6 chocolates

b) If Loraine then eats 4 chocolates, how many does she have left? (1)

Answer: 2 chocolates

12. Henry has 5 fewer marbles than Fiona, who has 11 marbles. How many marbles does Henry have? (1)

Answer: <u>6 marbles</u>

13. Solve the following: (9)

a) 8 x 2 = <u>16</u>

b) 3 x 5 = <u>15</u>

c) 6 lots of 6 = <u>36</u>

d) 4 multiplied by 7 = <u>28</u>

e) How many are nine fours? = <u>36</u>

f) How many 4s are there in 20? <u>5</u>

g) Divide 9 by 3 = <u>3</u>

h) Share 20 lollipops among 4 children = <u>5</u>

i) 65 ÷ 5 = <u>13</u>

This question aims to assess whether your child understands the different vocabulary associated with the multiplication and division signs.

Award one mark for each correct answer.

. . .

Model Answers & Guidance

14. There are 5 children on each basketball team

There are 5 teams in the league.

How many children are there in the league in total? (1)

5 x 5 = <u>25</u>

Answer: <u>25 children</u>

15. Toby needs to put his yo-yo collection into storage. He has 42 yo-yos. An empty shoe box can hold 6 yo-yos.

How many shoe boxes does Toby need to package up his entire collection? (1)

42 ÷ 6 = 7

7 shoe boxes.

The student may decide to draw out the problem in an array, or they may simply write out the calculation 42 ÷ 6 = 7.

Answer: <u>7 shoe boxes</u>

16. Daria has 9 conkers. Quinn has twice as many. How many conkers does Quinn have? (1)

9 x 2 = 18

<u>18 conkers</u>

Answer: <u>18 conkers</u>

17. Look at shapes A-F. (3)

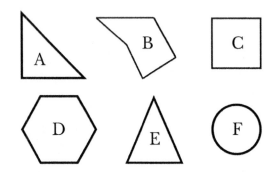

    a) Which is the pentagon?

A pentagon is a five-sided shape. However, not all five sides need to be of equal length. As a result, while it may not look like a regular pentagon, B is the correct answer.

Answer: <u>B</u>

    b) Which is the hexagon?

A hexagon is a six-sided shape.

Answer: <u>D</u>

    c) Which is the right-angled triangle?

Model Answers & Guidance

There are two triangles here: A and E. However, A is the one with a right angle (a 90 degree angle)

Answer: <u>A</u>

18. Shade half of this triangle: (1)

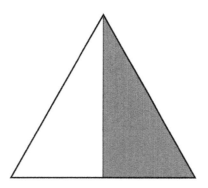

Award one mark for half the triangle being shaded correctly.

19.

a) Name 3 coins that add up to 22p (1)

Answer: <u>10p, 10p, and 2p OR 20p, 1p, 1p</u>

Award one mark for the correct response.

b) Name 3 coins that add up to 41p (1)

Answer: <u>20p, 20p, 1p</u>

Award one mark for the correct response.

20. Lawrence had two 50 pence coins. He spent 73p on a can of cola. How much change did he receive? (1)

27p

Your child might choose to mentally count on from 73p to £1 to find how much change Lawrence was given — or they might write out the following calculation:

100p - 73p = 27p

Award one mark for the correct answer.

Answer: 27p

21. How much is:

  a) Seven 5p coins and three 20p coins? (1)

35p + 60p = 95p

Answer: 95p

  b) Eight 2p coins and seven 10p coins? (1)

16p + 70p = 86p

Model Answers & Guidance

Answer: **86p**

22. Lucy and Leiliah decided to count their pocket money. (4)

a. Write the total underneath each piggy bank.

57p   75p

Award one mark for correctly counting and writing the total in each piggy bank.

b. Who has more money?

Leiliah

Award one mark for correctly saying Leiliah has more money.

Answer: **Leiliah**

c. How much more?

12p more

Award one mark for correctly calculating that Leiliah has 18p more than Lucy.

Answer: 12p more

d. How much do the children have in total?

75p + 57p = 132p

132p OR £1.32

Answer: 132p OR £1.32

---

23. Ada asked her classmates whether they prefer baths or showers, and kept a tally.

shower	baths

How many more people preferred a shower compared to those who preferred a bath? (1)

Model Answers & Guidance

Recap how many marks there are in each set that has a diagonal tally (=5) and how the student needs to count in 5s and then add on the individual tallies.

26 - 12 = <u>14</u>

Answer: <u>14</u>

24. Lance runs a YouTube channel.

The graph below shows how many views his most recent video received per day over the past week.

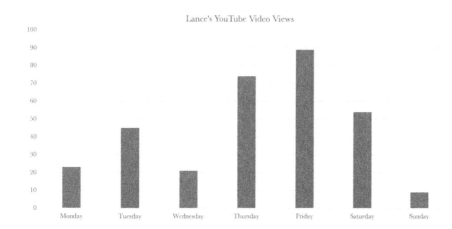

a) **On which day did Lance's video receive the most views? (1)**

Answer: <u>Friday</u>

b) **On which day did Lance's video receive the least views? (1)**

Answer: <u>Sunday</u>

25. Caroline runs a sauce shop.

Here is a graph representing the number of sales she made yesterday

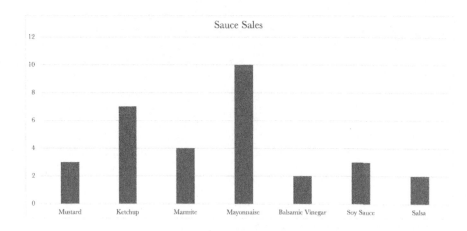

a) **How many units of marmite did she sell? (1)**

Answer: <u>4</u>

b) **How many units of ketchup did she sell? (1)**

Answer: <u>7</u>

Award one mark for each correct answer.

26. Look at the image below. (3)

a) **How many 'L' shapes are there?**

Model Answers & Guidance

Answer: 15

Award one mark for the correct answer.

b) How many 'C' shapes are there?

Answer: 6

Award one mark for the correct answer.

c) Are there more circles or more lines?

There are 6 lines, and 3 circles. As a result, there are more lines.

Answer: lines

27. Write the numbers shown on these abaci. (3)

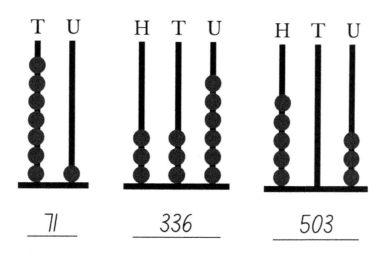

Recap with the student that the "H" stands for "Hundreds", the "T" stands for "Tens", and the "U" stands for "Units".

Printed in Great Britain
by Amazon